Meet

the

Evangelist

Meet

the

Evangelist

Joyce Vuyokazi Mrwetyana

authorHOUSE®

AuthorHouse™ UK Ltd.
1663 Liberty Drive
Bloomington, IN 47403 USA
www.authorhouse.co.uk
Phone: 0800.197.4150

NKJV
Scripture quotations marked NKJV are taken from the
New King James Version. Copyright © 1982 by Thomas
Nelson, Inc. Used by permission. All rights reserved.

Published by AuthorHouse 05/16/2014

ISBN: 978-1-4969-8096-0 (sc)
ISBN: 978-1-4969-8097-7 (e)

Library of Congress Control Number: 2014909143

DEDICATION

I want to dedicate this book to my grandmother Mrs. Caslina Nomantombazana Mrwetyana who thought me to be a woman of highest integrity and to my mother, a great woman of God, Elsie Nomahomba Mrwetyana.

To my two Aunts Nombulelo Miriam Mrwetyana and Mrs. Pastor Nompucuko Julia Dobe (sis Mpucu) who were good role models throughout my Christian life.

To my siblings Bro Mthetheleli and his wife Phindiwe, my sister Charity Nomveliso and my younger brother Thamsanqa.

To my two children, my son Abongile Themba who has been my pillar of strength throughout my entire life, and my daughter Mbalentle who has been my breeze of happiness.

To my other son and prayer warrior Luthando Bhili and to you, great woman of God, Pastor Emily Ezike, my friend.

Finally, to my spiritual leaders, Prophet Antony Imadojemu, whom God has used on my breakthrough and my spiritual upliftment and another great man of God, Pastor Agrippa Khathide, who has been of great help and motivation throughout this journey.

"To God Be the Glory"

Contents

A

Personal Testimony of Salvation

I received Christ some years ago. Before that my life was full of challenges: financially, spiritually and physically.

Financial Challenge

Before I was saved, I had a business which, in the beginning, was making money. Then things changed and I could not pay my workers or feed myself. I had a taxi bus which was making money for me and my family but, all of a sudden, it started to have many breakdowns and I ended up losing it. My other car was involved in an accident and another one was stolen. I could not run the business anymore and my friends advised that I go to a *sangoma*, as we suspected that a spiritual attack was causing the whole problem. So I traveled to Mozambique for help. Going there was not free and I had to use the last money I had, but there was no change. My truck, which I was using for driving school, was stolen while we were sleeping. Things got worse and I decided to look for a job. By the grace of God I found a job, and I'm still in the same one.

Spiritual and Physical Challenge:

During those challenges I started to be sick, thinking that there is no God. I got separated from my boyfriend. I got involved in an accident where I broke my leg. Things were out of control and I started to take alcohol, as it seemed like the only thing that could make me think better, although that was not really so.

Although I was busy with those things I had a spiritual man inside me saying, "God is the only solution".

One Sunday morning I went to visit another church. I'd been at a night club the previous night and I had a hangover, but I accompanied a friend to this Church. In that church the service was wonderful and I felt something move inside me and said to myself, "God is here and I am called".

The pastor who was ministering called for those who wanted to receive Jesus Christ as the saviour.

Something pushed me to stand and I stood up and made a covenant with Jesus Christ. Since that day I became a child of God. When I received Christ my attitude changed. I started to have a humble heart and also to show care towards other people. In *Rev 3:20* Jesus is standing at the door and knocking. If anyone hears His voice and opens the door, He will come in to him and dine with him, and he with Him.

Even when you are busy with your earthly things, Jesus is there waiting for you to open for Him. He cannot enter without you opening for Him.

In *Ephesians 2: 8-9* it says: for by grace we have been saved through faith, and not ourselves, it is the gift of God not of works, lest anyone should boast.

To me it is that grace of God that helped me during the journey of being carnal, doing things that were not pleasing to God. Despite that, God kept me until I received Him with my heart and soul. Were it not for that grace, I would be dead by now—Let God be the Glory. It is mentioned in *Romans 6:23* that the wages of sin is death, but the gift of God is eternal life in Christ Jesus our Lord.

ACCOUNT OF MY EVANGELISM EXPERIENCE SINCE CONVERSION:

Since I am a born-again Christian, I have a heart for converting people.

I started to talk about Christ to my friends and family.

I started to live as an example to those who have not received Christ as the Lord.

I joined evangelical groups in church and in the community, starting feeding schemes and taking care of disadvantage people, as well as going to hospital to pray for sick people.

Now my team and I are planning to start an outreach ministry, especially to those places where churches are fewer, so that everyone may receive the word of God.

We are registered under the department of Social services as CHRIST FOR ALL NATIONS HOME AND EVANGELISM INTL.

Pray to God that this program will win many souls for Jesus Christ to be glorified.

B   Prayer of Salvation

When a new believer accepts Christ as a saviour, pray this prayer:

> *Lord Come into My Life, Be My Lord, Be My Saviour.*
> *Today I Surrender My Life to You.*
> *Have Mercy on Me and Forgive My Sins*
> *Delete My Name from the Book of Death*
> *And Write My Name In the Book Of Life.*
> *Father God, Accept Me as Your Child.*
> *I Stand On the Word of God and Declare*
> *That I Am A Born Again Christian.*

1. Expectations of You, After Receiving Your Salvation

- Pray every day
- Read a Bible chapter e.g. Book of John
- Never be ashamed that you received Christ
- Join a fellowship group where you will grow spiritually.

2. Dealing With Temptation and Sin

What Is Sin?

- Sin is the *transgression of the law of God* (1 John 3:4) and *rebellion against God* (Deuteronomy 9:7; Joshua 1:18). It begins with Lucifer, probably the most beautiful and powerful of the angels. Not content with his position, he desired to be higher than God, and that was his downfall, the beginning of sin (Isaiah 14:12-15). Renamed Satan, he brought sin to the human race in the Garden of Eden, where he tempted Adam and Eve with the same enticement: "You shall be like God". (Romans 6:23). King David lamented this condition of fallen human nature in Psalm 51:5.

- Another type of sin is known as *imputed sin* and that is used in both financial and legal settings. It means "to take something that belongs to someone and credit it to another account" (Romans 5:13, 14; 1 John 2:2; 2 Corinthians 5:21).
- The third type of sin is *personal sin* which is committed every day by every human being. Because we have inherited a sinful nature from Adam, we commit individual, personal sins, everything from seemingly innocent untruths to murder. Those who have not placed their faith in Jesus Christ must pay the penalty for those personal sins, as well as inherited and imputed sin. However, believers have been freed from the eternal penalty of sin
- hell and spiritual death—and now we have the power to resist sinning (1 John 1:9, Romans 6:23; Revelation 20:11-15; Ephesians 1:7).
- There are various lists of sin (Proverbs 6:16-19; Galatians 5:19-21; 1 Corinthians 6:9-10). Make the most of every opportunity (Colossians 4:5, Ephesians 4:29).
- Everything that does not come from faith is sin (Romans 14:23; 1 Corinthian 6:19-20).

- We must evaluate our actions not only in relation to God, but also in relation to their effect on our families, our friends, and other people in general. Even if a particular thing may not hurt us personally, if it harmfully influences and affects someone else, then it is a sin (Romans 14:21, 15:1; 1 Cori. 6:12, Colossian 3:17).

3. *Watch Against Gossip*

What is gossip?

- Gossip is "idle talk; trifling or groundless rumour; tittle—tattle." A gossiper is a person who has, or pretends to have, privileged information about people and proceeds to reveal that information to those who have no business knowing it.
- Gossiping is distinguished from sharing information in two ways:

  1. INTENT: Gossipers often have the goal of building themselves up by making others look bad and exalting themselves as some kind of repositories of knowledge.
  2. THE TYPE OF INFORMATION SHARED: Gossipers speak of the faults and failing of others, or reveal potentially embarrassing or shameful details regarding the lives of others without their knowledge or approval. Even if they mean no harm, it is still gossip (Romans 1:29-32; 1 Timothy 5:12-13; Proverbs 11:12-13; 16:28; 18:7-8; 20:19; 21:23). So we must guard our tongues and refrain from the sinful act of

gossip. May we follow the Bible teaching on gossip by keeping our mouths shut unless it is necessary and appropriate to speak?

4. *Watch Against Jealousy*

What is jealousy?

- Jealousy is a sin. We use the word in a sense of being envious of someone who has something we do not have. It shows that we are still controlled by our desires (1 Corinthians 3:3; Galatians 5:26) "Let us not become conceited, provoking and envying each other".
- The Bible tells us that we are to have the perfect kind of love that Jesus has: "Love is Patient, Love is kind, it is not self-seeking, it is not easily angered, and it keeps no record of wrongs" (1 Corinthians 13:4-5). The more we focus on ourselves and our own desires, the less we are able to focus on God. When we harden our hearts to the truth, we cannot turn to Jesus and allow Him to heal us (Matthew 13:15). But when we allow the Holy Spirit to control us, He will produce in us the fruit of our salvation, which is love, joy, peace, patience, kindness, goodness, faithfulness, gentleness, and self-control (Galatians 5:22-23).
- Being jealous indicates that we are not satisfied with what God has given to us (Hebrews 13:5). In order to combat jealousy, we need to become more like Jesus and less like ourselves. We can get to know Him through Bible study, prayer, and fellowship with mature believers. As we learn to

serve others rather than ourselves, our hearts will begin to change. "Do not conform any longer to the pattern of this world, but be transformed by the renewing of your mind. Then You will be able to test and approve what God's will is his good, pleasing and perfect will" (Romans 12:2).

5. *Watch Anger*

What does the Bible say about anger?

- Anger can shatter communication and tear apart relationships, and ruins both the joy and health of many people. Sadly, people tend to justify their anger instead of accepting responsibility for it. Everyone struggles, to varying degrees, with anger. Thankfully, God's Word contains principles regarding how to handle anger in a Godly manner, and how to overcome sinful anger.
- Anger is not always sin: There is a type of anger of which the Bible approves, often called "righteous indignation". God is angry (Psalm 7:11; Mark 3:5), and believers are commanded to be angry (Ephesians 4:26). Biblically, anger is God-given energy intended to help us solve problems. Examples of Biblical anger include Paul's confronting Peter because of his wrong example (in Galatians 2:11-14), David's being upset when overhearing Nathan the Prophet sharing an injustice (2 Samuel 12) and Jesus at God's temple in Jerusalem (John 2:13-18). Notice that none of these examples of anger involve self-defence, but a defence of others or of a principle.

- Anger turns to sin: when it is selfishly motivated (James 1:20), when God's goal is distorted (1 Corinthian 10:31), or when anger is allowed to linger (Ephesians 4:26-27). Instead of using the energy generated by anger to attack the problem at hand, it is the person who is attacked. *Ephesians 4:15-19* says we are to speak the truth in love and use our words to build others up, not to allow rotten or destructive words to pour from our lips. Unfortunately, this poisonous speech is a common characteristic of fallen man (Romans 3:13-14). Anger becomes sin when it is allowed to boil over without restraint, resulting in a scenario with irreparable consequences. Anger also becomes sin when the angry one refuses to be pacified, holds a grudge, or keeps it all inside (Ephesians 4:26-27). This can cause depression and irritability over little things unrelated to the underlying problem.
- We can handle anger biblically by recognizing and admitting our selfish anger and / or our wrong handling of anger as sin (Proverb 28:13; 1 John 1:9). This confession should be both to God and to those who have been hurt by our anger. We should not minimize the sin by excusing it or blame-shifting.
- We can handle anger biblically by seeing God in the trial. This is especially important when people have done something to offend us. *James 1:2-4, Romans 8:28-29*, and *Genesis 50:20* all point to the fact that God is sovereign and in complete control over circumstance. Reflecting on this truth until it moves from our heads to our hearts will alter how we react to those who hurt us.

- We can handle anger biblically by making room for God's wrath. This is especially important in cases of injustice, when "evil" men abuse "innocent" people. *Genesis 50:19 and Romans 12:19* both tell us to not play God. God is righteous and just, and we can trust Him who knows all and sees all to act justly (Genesis 18:25).
- We can handle anger biblically by returning good for evil (Genesis 50:21; Romans 12:21). This is key to converting our anger into love. As our actions flow from our heart, so also our heart can be altered by our actions (Matthew 5:43-48). That is, we can change our feelings toward another by changing how we choose to act toward that person.
- We can handle anger biblically by communicating to solve the problem.

The four basic rules of communication shared in Ephesians 4:15, 25-32 are:

a) Be honest and speak (Ephesians 4:15, 25). People cannot read our minds. We must speak the truth in love.
b) Stay current (Ephesians 4:26-27). We must not allow what is bothering us to build up until we lose control. Dealing with and sharing what is bothering us before it gets to that point is important.
c) Attack the problem, not the person (Ephesians 4:29,31).

Along this line, we must remember the importance of keeping the volume of our voices low (Proverb 15:1).

d) Act, don't react (Ephesians 4:31-32). Because of our fallen nature, our first impulse is often a sinful one (v31). The time spent in "counting to ten" should be used to reflect upon the godly way to respond (v32) and to remind ourselves how anger is to be used to solve problems and not create bigger ones.

- Finally, we must act to solve our part of the problem (Romans 12:18). We cannot control how others act or respond, but we can make the changes that need to be made on our part. Overcoming a temper is not accomplished overnight. But through prayer, Bible study and reliance upon God's Holy Spirit, ungodly anger can be overcome. Just as we have allowed anger to become entrenched in our lives by habitual practice, we can practise responding correctly until it becomes a habit itself.

6. *When Somebody Does You Wrong: Luke 10:19; Matthew 6:6-15*

Somewhere along the way, we all get hurt or cheated or lied to or abused. It is as predictable as it is painful. Yet when it happens, most of us find ourselves strangely unprepared. In our outrage, we often cry out to God against the one who wronged us. We ask for justice, or even vengeance, and end up making things tougher on everyone involved—including ourselves.

If that has been true of you, it is time you found out how you can put the power of God to work for you the next time somebody does you wrong.

STEP ONE: Identify the enemy! Right here is where most of us make our biggest mistake. We mistakenly identify our enemy as the person who hurts us. Don't waste your energy ranting and raving or plotting and scheming against people who cause you pain. They are simply under the devil's influence. Aim your spiritual ammunition at the right target. It is the devil who is behind it all. Go after him!

STEP TWO: Fire! Once you have pointed your spiritual guns in the right direction, fire! Hit the devil fast and furiously with the word of God. Use the name of Jesus and the power that has been given you as a believer and bind the devil from doing you further harm in that area. Then move on to the next and most important part of this spiritual battle.

STEP THREE: Pray the prayer of intercession.

In *Matthew 5:44-45*, Jesus gives us these instructions: "Love your enemies, bless them that curse you, do good to them that hate you, and pray for them which despitefully use you, and persecute you; That you may be the children of your Father which is in Heaven."

Crying out for the vengeance of God to strike like a lightening bolt when somebody does us wrong is not acting like our Father.

Remember, God has great, great mercy. Not just for me and you, but for everyone!

The devil will probably think twice before he bothers you again. So, next time someone causes you pain, put the power of God to work for you. To summarize, identify the real enemy. Hit him hard with the authority you have been given as a believer. Then pray the prayer of intercession.

7. *Learn to Forgive*

LEAVE THE PAST BEHIND: Philippians 3:1-21

PHYSICAL FAILURES AND DISAPPOINTMENTS can be like aches and pains from the past that just don't seem to go away. Most of us know what it is like to suffer from them, but too few of us know what to do about them. So we limp along, hoping somehow they will magically stop hurting. But it never happens that way. Instead, as time goes by, things get worse—not better. Because, instead of putting those painful failures behind us, we often dwell on them until they become more real to us than the promises of God. Our problem is that we are forming our thoughts off the past instead of the future. Don't do that! Unbelief looks at the past and says, "See, it can't be done," but faith looks at the future and says, "It can be done, and according to the promises of God, it is done!" Then, putting past failures behind it forever, faith steps out and acts like the victory's already been won. If depression has driven you into a spiritual sudden fall, break out of it by getting your eyes off the past and onto your future—a future that has been guaranteed by Christ Jesus through the great and precious promises in His Word. Forget the past (Hebrews 8:12). God's mercies are new every morning. So, if you will take God at His Word, you can wake up every morning to a brand-new world. You can live life totally unhindered by the past.

SPIRITUAL BUMPS AND BRUISES that just don't seem to go away. The healing of a bruised and beaten spirit, however, does not come that easily. But there is a way out. All you have to do to break out of it is to get your eyes off the past and onto your future. Purposely meditate on the Word of God. Replace thoughts of the past with scriptural promises about your future and be diligent about it.

COME OUT OF SHADOW: John 1:29-34

Come out of the shadow of sin. Jesus came to take away sin. That means God, through the blood of Jesus, has so completely done away with the power of sin that you, as a born-again Christian, can live as if it never existed. You can step out from under its shadow once and for all.

LET PEACE RULE: Colossians 3:15, Psalm 95:1-7

Let the peace of Christ be your guide. Let it help you settle the issue that makes you not forgive. Watch out for strife. If you are irritated and upset about things in your life, it will be hard to receive that quiet guidance from the Holy Spirit. So take heed of the instructions at the end of the scripture and "Be

thankful . . . appreciative, giving praise to God always."
Maintain a thankful, grateful heart.

FREE YOUR FAITH: Mark 11:25, Matthew 18:21-35

Can you realize just how closely connected faith and forgiveness are? Jesus taught about that connection in His preaching on mountain—moving faith that is mentioned in Mark 11:22-26. Jesus wanted us to know that releasing those who have wronged us is fundamental to receiving from God. He wanted to make clear in our hearts the fact that we cannot have our prayers answered and hold grudges in our hearts at the same time. Unforgiveness blocks the faith channel and keeps you powerless against the mountains in your life. If you have been praying for something and you cannot get an answer, check your heart for unforgiveness. Ask the Holy Spirit to bring any grudge that is hidden there to light. Unblock the channel of faith and you will soon see things you have been praying for come to pass.

PROVE YOURSELF A SUCCESS: Luke 15:21-22, 32

Prove yourself at your work place and among friends. Even at home you must always work to win the approval you need. And there is only one place you can find it—in the heart of God Himself.

When you catch yourself struggling to make up to God for something you have done wrong, working to win His approval, let the story of the prodigal son set you free. Let it remind you that, in spite of your sins, your Father has received you with open arms. He has put a robe of righteousness on your back and His signet ring on your hand. He has put the shoes of son-ship on your feet!

Do you feel unworthy of all that? God has not based His relationship with you on your worthiness. He has based it on His love for you. You don't have to struggle to prove yourself to Him. As far as He is concerned you are a proven success.

SCRIPTURES FOR FORGIVENESS

Hebrews 8:12; Ephesians 4:32; Luke 6:37; 1 John 2:10-11; Matthew 5:23-24; Matthew 6:14-15; 1 John 3:21-22; Psalm 66:18; Mark 11:25

8. *Prayer of Love*

"Be a Living Example of Love": Romans 5:5

God's love is in you. What you need to do is make a decision to let it flow.

Pray This Prayer:

"In Jesus' Name, I make a fresh and strong commitment today to live a life of love, to let the tenderness of God flow through me and heal the wounded hearts of those I meet.

"Father, teach me to love even when things go wrong. To be patient and kind when the children are underfoot. To over- look the spiteful words of an angry spouse. To rejoice when someone at the office gets the raise that I thought I needed. Teach me to talk in love, to lay gossip quietly aside and to take up words of grace instead.

"Lord, your Word says that your love is already inside me . . .

That it has been shed abroad in my heart. So, today I resolve to remove every obstacle that would keep that love from flowing freely into the lives of others. I put resentments behind me, and I forgive all those who've done me wrong.

"In the days ahead, cause me to increase and excel and overflow with your love. Cause me to be what this world needs most of all . . . a living example of love. Amen."

9. Scriptures for Love:

1. Believe The Love: 1 John 4:16; Psalms 139:1-18
2. Love Is The Power Charge: John 15:12-13; 1 Corinthians 13:1-8
3. Peace At Home: James 3:16; Philippians 2:1-13
4. A Covenant Of Love: John 3:16; Genesis 15
5. That Your Prayers May Not Be Hindered: 1 John 1:7; Romans 15:1-7
6. Leaving The Pain Behind: 1 Corinthians 13:5; Luke 6:27-37
7. Live The Love Life: 1 John 2:5-6; 1 Corinthians 13:1-13
8. No Offence: 1 John 2:10; 1-11
9. The Father's Heart: Luke 15:20; John 8:1-11
10. Develop The Love: 2 John 1:6; 1 John 2:3-11
11. A Healthy Dose Of Love: 1 Corinthians 13:4-5; Proverbs 4:10
12. Protected By Love: Matthew 5:44-45; Matthew 5:38-48

C   Discipleship

1. What is Evangelism?

Evangelism is the preaching of the Christian gospel or the practice of relaying information about a particular set of beliefs to others with the object of conversion.

Evangelism is usually regarded as converting non-Christians to Christianity,

2. What is an Evangelist?

Those Christians who specialize in evangelism are known as evangelists.

3. How do we Evangelize?

When Lord Jesus Christ sent His disciples to evangelize, the gospel says: "and he called the twelve to *himself,* and began to send them out two by two, and gave them power over unclean spirit. He commanded them to take nothing for the journey except a staff—no bag, no bread, and no copper in their money belts, but to wear sandals, and not to put on two tunics (Mark 6:7-11).

This suggests that it is better to have at least one other person working with you in evangelism than to work by yourself.

a. *What Is The Role Of A Church Work In A Church?*

i. **Prepare The Church To Receive Guests:**

- There are many things that you could do here. First, m*ake sure the church is clean*. Make sure there are no empty cans or other trash in the yard of the church and that the rest rooms are clean and have enough paper towels and soap. Then check that:
- *the thermometer/fan is set at a reasonable temperature*. Too much cold and too much heat can chase away the visitors
- *the microphone of the church is set at a reasonable volume*. Some choir members love to set microphones at a high volume and sing very close to the microphone, which make it uncomfortable to listen to.
- *the chairs of the church are clean.*
- *there are enough prayer books* and there is a screen that shows the page number of the prayer book, that it works, and there is at least one person who can operate it.
- It is a great idea to encourage the church to buy the software that shows on screens all the prayer and the readings.

ii. **During Service**

- There should be at least one person who stands at the door to *welcome any guest.*
- *Prepare small cards for the guest to fill* out their names, e-mail addresses, and their telephone numbers.

- *Meet the guest with a smile and welcoming words.*

  Introduce yourself and welcome them in the name of the church. Ask them politely to fill out the cards so the church can also welcome them.
- *Give each guest a prayer book*, tell them about the screen, and ask them if they need someone to help them follow the prayers. If the answer is yes, ask someone to stand next to them to help.
- *Prepare them for our fire prayer*: tell them briefly that the worship and prayer is biblical. Therefore, it can be different from what they know/what they may be accustomed to. Nevertheless, it is very rich in spirituality. Tell them we stand up most of the time, but they should feel free to sit.
- *Lead each person to where he or she will sit down.*

  Please avoid seating them at the very rear of the church because usually this area has more noisy children. Also, avoid seating them up where they could feel uncomfortable since everybody can see their unfamiliarity in following the prayers. Please don't let them to sit next to the loud speaker!
- *Prepare the list of guest's names and give them to the pastor* to welcome them publicly from the pulpit.
- Make sure that there is a *translation for the sermon*.
- Let the pastor knows that there are guests, so he can pray more in their language.

iii. After Service

- *Welcome guests again and express your desire to see them again the following week.* This will help them feel accepted and welcomed.
- If they have time, **lead them to the coffee room** and make sure that you help them around.
- **Introduce them to others** and ask people to spend time with them and let them feel welcomed and accepted. Also, ask those people to let the guests know that they enjoyed their company and that they also would like to see them again the following week.
- **Introduce them to the pastor** to welcome them personally and spend a few moments with each. Guests consider the pastor as the manger of the church; therefore his welcome is very important to them.
- During the week, **call the guest** and thank them for coming and invite them to come again.
- *Give their name to the Bible study group.*
- Add their names to the list of people the evangelism group should pray for.

D

Becoming A Disciple

1. Live A Christian Life

What is the Christian life supposed to be?

- A Christian life is supposed to be a life lived by faith. It is by faith that we enter into the Christian life, and it by faith that we live it out. When we begin the Christian life by coming to Christ for forgiveness of sin, we understand that what we seek cannot be obtained by any other means than by faith. The Bible clearly teaches: "but that no one is justified by the law in the sight of God is clear, for, 'the just shall live by his faith'" (Galatians 3:11). The gospel of Christ actually reveals God to us as we live to grow closer to him each day. *Romans 1:17* says, "for in the gospel a righteousness from God is revealed, a righteousness that is by faith from first to last, just as is written: 'the righteous will live by faith'", so part of the Christian life is diligent reading and study of the word, accompanied by prayer for understanding and wisdom and for a closer, more intimate relationship with God through the Holy Spirit.
- The Christian life is also supposed to be one of death to self in order to live a life by faith (Galatians 2:20, 2 Corinthians 5:17).
- The Christian life is also supposed to persevere to the end (Hebrews 10:38-39, Ephesians 1:13-14

- So, the Christian life is one lived by faith in the God who saved us, empowers us, seals us for heaven, and by whose power we are kept forever. The day-by-day life of faith is one that grows and strengthens as we seek God in His word and through prayer and as we unite with other Christians whose goal of Christ-likeness is similar to our own.

2. Be a Prayer Warrior

What Is a Prayer Warrior?

- A Prayer Warrior is a person who prays continually and effectively for others in the manner of praying taught in scripture.
- Therefore they pray to Father God (Matthew 6:9).
- To be a prayer warrior in prayer is to engage in the spiritual battle and fight the good fight of faith, wearing the full armour of God and praying in the spirit on all occasions with all kinds of prayers and requests (Ephesians 6:10-18).
- All believers in Christ have the Holy Spirit who helps us communicate our prayer request (Romans 8:26-27).
- We pray in the name of Jesus, which means that Jesus Christ is our lord and saviour, that we must trust in Him for everything, including His interceding with the Father God for us in all things, and that we live and pray in accordance with God's will.
- Praying in Jesus' name does not mean merely adding "in Jesus' name" to a prayer. Rather, it means praying in submission to His will.

- As a prayer warrior, we rejoice in all things and have a spirit of thankfulness for what God is doing in our lives and in the lives of others, and our own spirit grows day by day as we come to realize the magnitude of our blessings.
- We know with certainty that God provided the breath we just took (Isaiah 42:5); that He has forgiven our past, present and future sin (1 John 2:12); that He loves us with eternal love (Ephesians 2:4-7) and that we have a place in heaven with our Lord (1 Peter 1:3-5). Our hearts, then, are filled with joy and peace and overflow with love for God, and we want others to have this same love, joy and peace. Therefore we work for them by praying.
- Effective prayer is indeed work.
- We have to learn to walk with God, so we meditate daily on Him and His ways in order to become more and more humble, an essential for effective prayers (2 Chronicles 7:13-15).
- We also study scripture thoughtfully every day to learn what constitutes acceptable prayer.
- We learn to eliminate hindrances to prayer (Mark 11:25, 1 Peter 3:7, 1 John 3:21-22) and not to grieve the spirit of God (Ephesians 4:30-32).
- We learn that we are in spiritual battle with Satan so we must pray for our own spiritual wellbeing to maintain our strength and focus in pray for Christ church.
- We pray continually and trust that God answers each prayer according to His perfect will and in His perfect timing.

3. Be a Preacher

How can you know if you are called to preach?

- There is no doubt that preaching is a noble calling and one which is far more important to God than it is to most people. Preaching is not simply a time-filler in the worship service, nor is it the sharing of personal experiences, no matter how emotional. Preaching, as the apostle Paul records, is the vehicle by which the life-giving truth of the gospel of Jesus Christ is conveyed.
- The words of the preacher are to be faithful to the word of God which is "the power unto salvation for everyone who believes" (Romans 1:16). Paul's admonition to the young pastor Timothy was, "in the presence of God and of Christ Jesus . . . I give you this charge: preach the word . . . !" (2 Timothy 4:1-2). So there is no doubt the preaching of the word is of primary importance to God, and so must it be for anyone considering entering the ministry as pastor.

How can one be sure a person is called to preach?

- First are the subjective indicators. If a man has the burning desire within him that cannot be denied, that is a good indication of a "calling" by God. The apostle Paul and old testament prophet Jeremiah experienced the same desire. Paul said, "yet when I preach the gospel, I cannot boast, for I am compelled to preach. Woe to me if I do not preach the gospel!"(1 Corinthians 9:16). To be compelled to preach means to be driven onward by an irresistible and undeniable compulsion to do so. Jeremiah described it as a "burning fire" (Jeremiah 20:8-9) that could not be stifled. Trying to hold it back made him weary.

- Second, there are objective indicators of God's calling to preach. If the response to early efforts at preaching are positive, this is a good indication that the prospective preacher has the gift of teaching from the Holy Spirit (Ephesians 4:11). Every preacher must be first and foremost a teacher of God's word, conveying it in a clear and concise manner and making personal application to the hearers. The church leadership are usually the best determiners of whether a man has this gift. If they are agreed that he does, the prospective preacher should then be examined by leadership as to character, as outlined in the requirements for elders (1 Timothy. 3, Titus 1).

- Finally, the whole process should be bathed in prayer every step of the way. If God is truly calling a man to preach, He will confirm it in many ways. Seek His face and ask that doors are opened to more opportunities and more confirmations, both internal and external. Ask also that doors will close if it is not His will to continue. Take heart in the fact that God is sovereign and in control of all things and will work "all things . . . Together for good to those who love God, to those who are called according to his purpose" (Romans 8:28). If He has called you, that call will not be denied.

4. Be Submissive to Your Leaders

A Leader is any individual who has a spiritual authority over another individual.

- It is good to have confidence in your leaders and to submit to their authority, because they keep watch over you as those who must give an account. Do this so that their work will be a joy, not a burden, for that would be of no benefit to you (Hebrews 13:17).
- Yes, the Bible very clearly states that God gives some individuals spiritual authority over others. There are various levels of authority in any person's life, and each of these levels may involve different people in different positions of authority. Of course, we must begin with the highest authority, which is God. *Genesis 1:1* states "in the beginning God created the heaven and earth". Everything that exists was created by God and, by that fact, God has ultimate authority, or sovereignty, over all things. When Moses delivered the law to the Israelites, God's sovereign authority was the basis on which they were to submit to it (Deuteronomy 4:39-40, Job 9:1-12, Genesis 14:22, Acts 17:24, Matthew 28:18).
- One level of authority that God has granted to men is civil or governmental. *Romans 13:1-6* states that "the powers that be are ordained of God" (Colossians 3:22-24).
- Another level of authority established by God is within the home. *Ephesians 5:22-24* commands wives to submit to their husbands as they would

submit to God (1 Corinthians 11:3; Ephesians 6:1; Colossians 3:20).

- God established authority within the church. As Christians, we are all joint heirs with Christ (Romans 8:17) and have full access to God by the Holy Spirit (Ephesians 2:18). Though God is no respecter of persons (Romans 2:11), He has chosen to place some in positions of authority for the sake of order and growth (Ephesians 4:11-13). The early church recognized the authority of the apostles and submitted to their teaching and direction (Acts 6:2, 15:2, Acts 14:23, 1 Peter 5:1-3). Spiritual leaders have a greater responsibility to God (James 3:1) and must meet the qualifications God has established (Titus 1:5-9; 1 Timothy 3:1-7). Believers are told to acknowledge and respect those who are over them in spiritual matters (1 Thessalonians 5:12-13) and even to support them financially (Timothy 5:17-18; 1 Peter 5; 5-6, Mark 9:35, Philippians 2:7-11.

5. The Importance of Christian Conduct to the Unbelievers

This is very important! The Bible is supplied with the verses that link Christian conduct with how the world sees Christ. "In the same way, let your light shine before others, so that they may see your good works and give glory to your father who is in heaven" (Matthew 5:16). "By the approval of this service, they will glorify God because of your submission that comes from your confession of the gospel of Christ, and the generosity of your contribution for them and for all others" (2 Corinthians 9:13). "Keep your conduct among the gentiles honourable, so that when they speak against you as evildoers, they may see your good deeds and glorify God on the day of visitation" (1 Peter 2:12).

- When unbelievers see the love Christians have for one another and the good works they perform, they may think all sorts of evil things about Christians, but they cannot fault their conduct and this abounds to the glory of God. Even in our witnessing and defence of the faith, we should conduct ourselves with gentleness and respect (1 Peter 3:15), not in anger, or in boastful tones.
- The truth of the matter is that the gospel is already an offence to the unbelieving world (1 Corinthians 1:18); Christians should not add to the offence. This sentiment is clearly seen in Peter's first epistle. He exhorts his readers to, if they're going to suffer at the hands of evil men, let it be because they are Christians and not because they were acting sinfully (1 Peter 4:14-16).
- (Titus 2:5, 2:7-8, 2:9-10) If Christians conduct themselves no differently from the outside world, what good is that? (1 Corinthians 2:14, Romans 8:7-8). The gospel is much more likely to be received positively if it is presented by a person who is humble and gentle than a person who is rude and cantankerous. Our actions can either help or hinder the gospel.

6. Honour or Esteem or Value or Have Great Respect for Someone

- To honour someone is to value them highly or bestow value upon them. The Bible exhorts us to express honour and esteem toward certain people: our parents, the aged, and those in authority (Ephesians 6:2; Leviticus 19:32; Romans 13:1) but we must understand that all authority and honour belong to God alone (1 Chronicles 29:11; 1 Timothy 1:17; Revelation 5:13). Though He can delegate His authority to others, it still belongs to Him (Ephesians 4:11-12).
- Peter tells us to; "honour all people, love the brotherhood, fear God, honour the king (1 Peter 2:17). The idea of honouring others, especially those who are in authority (the king), comes from the fact that they represent God's ultimate authority. A classic example is the command to "submit to the governing authorities because they have been established by God" (Romans 13:1-6). Therefore, "he who rebels against the authority is rebelling against what God has instituted, and those who do so will bring judgment on themselves" (Romans 13:2). This means it is incumbent upon Christians to honour those whom the lord has placed over us through our obedience and demonstration of respect.
- The scripture speaks of another noteworthy group of people who are deserving of "double honour": the leadership of the church, called elders (1 Timothy 5:17).

- The scripture also gives us the command to honour one another in our employer/employee relationships (1 Timothy 3:1-7,6:1; Ephesians 6:5-9), as well as in the marriage relationship with the husband and wife being in submission to and honouring one another "as Christ loved the church and gave Himself up for her (Hebrews 13:4; Ephesians 3:2-3; Exodus 20: 12; Matthew 15:4; Exodus 21:7
- The word "love" is also sometimes synonymous for honour. (Romans 12:10, 12:3; Philippians 2:3; Proverbs 21:21; 22:4; 29:23; 1 Kings 10:6-7; Joshua 6:27; Ecclesiastes 1:14; James 4:14).

7. *Handling Discrimination, Racism and Prejudice*

How can we handle discrimination?

- There is only one race—the human race. All human beings have the same physical characteristics (with minor variations, of course). More importantly, all human beings are created in the image and likeness of God (Genesis 1:26-27). God loved the world so much that He sent Jesus to lay down His life for us (John 3:16). The "world" obviously includes all ethnic groups.
- God does not show partiality or favouritism (Deuteronomy 10:17; Acts 10:34; Romans 2:11; Ephesians 6:9), and neither should we. *James 2:4* describes those who discriminate as "judges with evil thoughts". Instead, we are to love our neighbours as ourselves (James 2:8). Jesus Christ put an end to enmity, destroying the dividing wall

of hostility (Ephesians 2:14). All forms of racism, prejudice and discrimination are affronts to the work of Christ on the cross.

- Jesus commands us to love one another as He love us (John 13:34). If God is impartial and loves us with impartiality, then we need to love others with that same high standard. Jesus teaches, in *Matthew 25*, that whatever we do to the least of His brothers, we do to Him. If we are treating a person with contempt, we are mistreating a person created in God's image and we are hurting somebody whom God loves and for whom Jesus died (Ephesians 4:32, Romans 6:13, Galatians 3:28).

8. Practise Hospitality

What is hospitality?

- Hospitality is "the quality or disposition of receiving and treating guests and strangers in a warm, friendly, generous way". Hospitality is a virtue which is both commanded and commended throughout scripture. In the old testament, it was specifically commanded by God: "when an alien lives with you in your land, do not mistreat him. The alien living with you must be treated as one of your native-born. Love him as yourself, for you were alien in Egypt (Leviticus 19:33-34).
- During His public ministry, Jesus and His disciples depended entirely on the hospitality of others as they ministered from town to town (Matthew 10:9-10, Acts 2:44-45; 28:7). This generous provision

to strangers also included opening one's home for church services (Titus 1:8; 1 Timothy 3:2).

- The book of Hebrews reminds us not to forget to "entertain strangers, for by so doing some people have entertained angels without knowing it" (Hebrews 13:2; Genesis 18: 1-8).

- Christians are "God's workmanship, created in Christ Jesus to do good works" (Ephesians 2:10). As followers of Christ, we emulate His love and compassion when we show hospitality, not only to fellow Christians, but even more so to strangers and the less fortunate. In fact, we honour God when we are kind to the needy (Proverbs 14:31, 19:17). As Jesus said, when you give a banquet, invite the poor, the crippled, the lame and the blind, and you will be blessed" (Luke 14:13). Christ also taught us the second commandment, to "love your neighbour as your self" (Matthew 22:39) and the parable of the good Samaritan teaches us that "neighbour" has nothing to do with geography, citizenship, or race. Wherever and whenever people need us, there we can be neighbours and, like Christ, show mercy. This is the essence of hospitality.

- In the gospel of Matthew, Jesus discusses the hospitable behaviour of those who will inherit the kingdom. "For I was hungry and you gave me something to eat, I was thirsty and you gave me something to drink, I was a stranger and you invited me in, I needed clothes and you clothed me, I was sick and you looked after me, I was in prison and you came to visit me" (Matthew 25:34-36). In these days we often don't think much about entertaining strangers, but hospitality is still an important part of Christian ministry (Romans 12:13; 1 peter 4:9). By serving others we serve Christ (Matthew 25:40) and we promote the spread of God's truth (3 John: 5-8).

9. Is There Food a Christian Should Avoid?

In the book of Leviticus, chapter 11 has listed the dietary restrictions God gave to the nation of Israel. Those dietary laws included prohibitions against eating pork, shrimp, shellfish and many types of seafood, most insects, scavenger birds and various other animals.

- Those dietary rules were never intended to apply to anyone other than the Israelites. The purpose of the food laws was to make the Israelites distinct or different from all other nations. After this purpose had ended, Jesus declared all foods clean (Mark 7:19). God gave the apostle Peter a vision in which He declared that formerly unclean animals could be eaten: "Do not call anything impure that God has made clean" (Acts 10:15). When Jesus died on the cross, He fulfilled the Old Testament law (Romans 10:4; Galatians3:24-26; Ephesians 2:15) and this includes the laws regarding clean and unclean foods.
- Romans 14:1-23 teaches us that not everyone is mature enough in the faith to accept the fact that all foods are clean. AS A RESULT, if we are with someone who would be offended by our eating "unclean" food, we should give up our right to do so, so as not to offend the other person. We have

the right to eat whatever we want, but we do not have the right to offend other people, even if they are wrong. For us as Christians of these days, though, we have freedom to eat whatever we wish as long as it does not cause some one else to tumble in his or her faith.

- In The New Covenant of grace, the *Bible is far more concerned with how much we eat than what we eat.* If we are not able to control our eating habits, we are probably also unable to control other habits such as those of the mind (lust, covetousness, unrighteous hatred or anger) and unable to keep our mouths from gossip or strife. We are not to allow our appetites to control us; rather, we are to control them (Deuteronomy 21;20; Proverb 23:2; 2 Peter 1:5-7; 2 Timothy 3:1-9; 2 Corinthians 10:5).

E

Dress Code

1. Why Do We Have to Dress up Nicely for Church?

- It is good for us to consider why we wear what we do. Genesis 35:1-3 give us some light on the subject. "Then God said to Jacob, 'Go up to Bethel and settle there. Build an altar there to honour me. That's where I appeared to you when you were running away from Brother Esau.' So Jacob spoke to his family and to everyone who was with him. He said, 'Get rid of the strange gods you have with you. Make yourself pure, and change your clothes. Come, let's go up to Bethel. There I'll build an altar to honour God. He answered me when I was in trouble. He's been with me everywhere I've gone.'"

- When Jacob began this faith-journey to Bethel with God, he recognized how much God had done for him, and how much he needed God! His response was to take everyone with him on this faith-journey, so they could experience God for themselves. "Get rid of the strange Gods you have with you. Make yourselves pure" implies the need to be united in "coming clean" before God. "For all have sinned . . ." (Romans 3:23). Many then had "household idols" with them, that they depended on, as well as God. They did not trust God alone. "Change your clothes" implies a change of heart toward sin. It was to be an external reflection of what had taken place on the "inside".

- We would all benefit from a "SPIRITUAL BATH" to confess and get rid of sin before we go to church. This makes us pure. For some people, clean is their "best". For others, their heart tells them that wearing their best is showing God His value to them. For still others, there needs to be a caution that their best isn't merely showing off.
- It is always the heart God is looking at, rather than the exterior. However, what we wear to worship our holy, pure God may be an indication of where our hearts are. If you have never considered it before, ask yourself, "Does it matter to me how I look when I am going to worship the King of kings and Lord of lords? More importantly, does it matter to Him?" We must all be the judge of that for ourselves. It is a personal choice, keeping in mind that having a proper attitude toward God Himself is important preparation for worship at church.

2. *What Does it Mean to Dress Modestly?*

- In describing the mode of dress appropriate for women in church, the apostle Paul urges them to dress "MODESTLY, with DECENCY and PROPRIETY" and then goes on to contrast immodest dress with the good deeds which are appropriate for those who profess to be the standard for all Christians at all times. The key to understanding what constitutes modesty in dress is to examine the attitudes and intents of the heart. Those whose hearts are not inclined toward God will make every effort to dress in a manner designed to draw attention to themselves with little or no regard for the consequences to themselves or others.

- A Godly woman endeavours to do everything with a "God-ward" perspective. She knows that God wants His people to be concerned for His glory and the spiritual state of their brothers and sisters in Christ. If a woman professes to be a Christian and yet she dresses in a way that will unduly draw attention to her body, she is a poor witness of the One who bought her soul by dying for her on the cross. She is forgetting that her body has been redeemed by Christ and is now the TEMPLE of the HOLY SPIRIT (1 Corinthian 6:19-20). She is telling the world that she sees her own worth as purely physical and that her attractiveness to others depends on how much of her body she reveals to them. Further, by dressing in an immodest fashion, displaying her body for men to lust after, she causes her brothers in Christ to sin, something condemned by God (Matthew 5:27-29). Proverbs 7:10 mentions a woman "dressed like a prostitute and with crafty intent". Here we see the description of one whose heart condition is displayed by her manner of dress.

- The scripture says that woman is to dress modestly, but what exactly does that mean in modern society? Does a woman have to be covered from head to toe? There are cults and religions in the world that demand this of women. But is that the biblical meaning of modesty? Again, we have to go back to the matter of the attitudes of the heart. If a woman's heart is inclined toward godliness, she will wear clothing that is neither provocative nor revealing in public, clothing that does not reflect negatively upon her personal testimony as a child of God. Even when everyone else in her circle is dressing immodestly, she resists the temptation to go along with the crowd. She knows these types of clothes are designed to draw attention to her body and cause men to lust after her, but she is wise enough to know that that type of attention only cheapens her. The idea of causing men to sin against God because of her dress is abhorrent to her because she seeks to love and honour God and wants others to do the same. Modesty in dress reveals a modesty and godliness of the heart, attitudes that should be the desire of all women who live to please and honour God.

3. Should Christian Women Wear Head Coverings?

- The issue of women and head coverings is addressed in 1 Corinthian 11:3-16. The context of the entire passage of 1 Corinthians 11:3-16 is submission to the God-given order and "chain of command." A "covering" on a woman's head is used as an illustration of order, headship, and the authority of God. The key verse of this passage is 1 Corinthians 11:3: "But I want you to know that the head of every man is Christ, the head of woman is man, and the head of Christ is God." The order is: God the father, God the Son, the man or husband, and the woman or wife. The veil or covering on the head of a believing Corinthian wife showed that she was under the authority of her husband, and therefore under submission to God.

- Within this passage is also verse 10: "For this reason, the woman ought to have a symbol of authority on her head, because of the angels." Why is that important to angels? The relationship of God with men is something that angels watch and learn from (1 Peter 1:12). Therefore, a woman's submission to God's delegated authority over her is an example to angels. The holy angels, who are in perfect and total submission to God, expect that we, as followers of Christ, be the same.
- This covering not only means a cloth but can also refer to a woman's hair length. How can we say that? We must take this verse in the context or the setting in which it is presented. "Does not even nature itself teach you that if a man has long hair, it is a dishonour to him? But if a woman has long hair, it is a glory to her; for her hair is given to her for a covering" (1 Corinthian 11: 14-15). The roles of the male and female are designed by God to portray a profound spiritual lesson, that is of submission to the will and order of God.
- But why is hair an issue in this passage? The Apostle Paul is addressing something in the Corinthian culture that was being to allowed to disrupt the church. Paul says in this passage that a woman who is shorn or shaved should be covered (1 Corinthian 11:6), for a woman shorn or shaved of her hair had lost her "glory", and she was not under the protection of a husband. A shorn or shaved head without a covering was equivalent to saying, "I refuse to submit to God's order". Therefore, the apostle Paul is teaching the Corinthians that hair length, or wearing of a "covering" by the woman,

was an outward indication of heart attitude of submission to God and His established authority. This was important because the Corinthian church was to be separate from the corrupt pagan culture of Corinth (2 Corinthians 6:17).

- God's order is that the husband is the head of the wife as God is the head of Christ, but there is no inequality or inferiority implied. God and Christ are equal and united, just as the husband and the wife are one. This is not a passage that teaches that the woman is inferior to man or that she should be submissive to every man. It is teaching God's order and spiritual headship in the marriage relationship. In Corinthian culture, a woman who covered her head during worship or when she was in public displayed her submission to authority.

4. Should Christian Women Wear Pants?

- The obedience of a child of God is not measured by what clothing we wear but by our walk in the Spirit (Galatians 5:16).
- There is passage in the Old Testament that speaks about a woman wearing men's clothing: "A woman must not wear men's clothing, or a man wear women's clothing, for the Lord your God detests anyone who does it" (Deuteronomy 22:5). The context of this passage is the second giving of the law to the nation of Israel as they were poised to enter the Promised Land. *Deuteronomy 22:5* is an admonition not to live as transvestites. This has to do with more than just clothing; it also speaks of a life that emulates in every way those

of the opposite sex. Transvestism was a practice of the Canaanites, and Israel was to consider it an abomination. We take a principle from this and apply it to our lives as believers, but we must use it in the context in which it is given and do so in relation to the dispensation of grace. Apostle Paul said we are not justified by our adherence to the law, but we are justified by faith in Christ (Romans 3:21-28 and Romans 7:6). Therefore, a believer does not live by legalism, nor by license, but rather by grace.

- What has that to do with a believing woman wearing pants? There is no biblical law that says what a woman should wear or not wear. Rather, the issue is one of MODESTY. Paul addresses the modesty of women in his first letter to Timothy. "I also want women to dress modestly, with decency and propriety, not with braided hair or gold or pearls or expensive clothes, but with good deeds, appropriate for women who profess to worship God" (1 Timothy 2:9-10). Paul addressed this issue here because the women in the church were trying to outdo each other in how they dressed and the flashier the better. They were losing sight of the thing that should adorn a Godly woman—humility.

5. *Should a Christian Wear Religious Jewelry?*

- Christians did not begin wearing crosses around their necks until after crucifixion was no longer the primary source of capital punishment; therefore, it is not the equivalent to a modern-day person wearing a miniature death chamber around his neck. Many look at the cross as simply the instrument of death used to slay our beloved Saviour. Because it was God's will, Jesus willingly went to the cross, taking upon Himself the sins of the world, cleansing those who believe in Him of their own sins

- The only reason scripture would the forbid wearing a cross or crucifix would be if the object became an idol used for worship (1 Corinthians 10:14) or if the wearer were consumed with how the jewellery made her look (1 Peter 3:3). Many Christians wear crosses as a proud expression of their love, respect and service to Christ, along with a remembrance of what HE DID FOR US.

- Another concern is when people allow objects such as crosses, crucifixes, rosaries, bumper stickers and so on to take the place of the true change that should take place in our hearts. The things we wear, carry, or put on our cars are not what make us Christians. God is not concerned with what we wear so long as we do not dress in a way that would cause anyone to stumble in his or her walk with God (Romans 14:20) and we are not absorbed with our looks or our possessions. He is searching out our hearts to find who is faithful to Him and whether we encourage and show love to others. It is not for any of us to judge whether wearing a cross is proper or not; every Christian has to seek God's approval in all he does. If it is not clearly outlined in scripture whether a practice is lawful or edifying, then the practice is one better left to each person's conscience.

F   Pitfalls in Relationships

1. What is the Purpose of Marriage?

- Since the first marriage was between the first man and first woman, it is assumed that marriage is God's will for most people.
- It was instituted "in the time of man's innocence" and is therefore a holy institution.
- The reason for the existence of marriage is simple: Adam was lonely and needed a helper (Genesis 2:18). This is the primary purpose of marriage—fellowship, companionship, and mutual help and comfort.
- One purpose of marriage is to create a stable home in which children can grow and thrive.
- The best marriage is between two believers (2 Corinthians 6: 14) who produce Godly children (Malachi 2:13-15).
- The children of faithful people will tend to be faithful too.
- Marriage has a sanctifying effect on both marriage partners when they submit to God's law (Ephesians 5).
- Marriage is very helpful for one trying to live a Godly life: it helps to scrub the heart clean of selfishness and other impurities.
- Marriage also protects individuals from sexual immorality (1 Corinthians 7:12). Marriage provides a healthy place to express sexuality.

- It is clear that God created marriage for our good (Proverbs 18:22), to make us happy, to promote a healthier society, and to produce holiness in our lives.
- Marriage is a beautiful picture of the relationship between Christ and His church (Ephesians 5:25-26, Revelations 19:7-9; 21:1-2).

1.1 What Should You be Looking for in a Husband?

- When a Christian woman is looking for a husband, she should seek a man "after God's own heart" (Acts 13:22). The potential husband should be a man who has his focus upon walking in obedience to God's Word and who seeks to live so that his life brings glory to God (1 Corinthians 10:31).
- The qualities to look for in a husband are as follows: a man should be patient and controlled in his way of conduct, not filled with pride but of sober mental attitude, able to master his emotions, given to graciousness to others, able to patiently teach, not given to drunkenness or uncontrolled use of any of God's gifts, not prone to violence, not overly focused upon the details of life but focused upon God, not so short-tempered a man that he takes offence easily, and grateful for what God has given, rather than envious of what gifts others have received.
- That is the type of man a woman should look for as a potential husband.
- Yes, physical attraction, similar interests, complementary strengths and weaknesses, and the desire for children are also things to consider.

- That your husband should be a man you trust, respect, and follow in the path of Godliness is of far greater value than a man of good looks, fame, power, or money.
- Finally, when "looking" for a husband, we must be surrendered to God's will in our lives. We must enter into the second most important relationship of our lives (marriage), not under an emotional cloud, but with eyes wide open.
- Our most important relationship, with our Lord and Saviour, has to be the focus of our lives.

1.2 What is the key to making marriage last?

- The first and most important issue is one of obedience to God and His Word. This is the principle that should be in force before the marriage. God says they should "not walk together unless they have agreed to do so" (Amos 3:3). A born-again believer shouldn't start a close relationship with anyone who is not also a believer: "do not be yoked together with unbelievers, for what do righteousness and wickedness have in common? Or what fellowship can light have with darkness? (2 Corinthians 6:14).
- Another principle that would protect the life of a marriage is that the husband should obey God and love, honour, and protect his wife as he would his own body (Ephesians 5:25-31). Also, the wife should obey God and submit to her own husband "as to the Lord" (Ephesians 5:22). The marriage between a man and a woman is a picture of the relationship between Christ and the Church (Revelation 19:7-9).

- When God brought Adam and Eve together in the first marriage, she was made from his "flesh and bone" (Genesis 2:21) and they become "one flesh" (Genesis 2:23-24). Becoming one means more than just a physical union. This relationship goes far beyond sexual and emotional attraction and into the realm of spiritual "oneness" that can only be found as both partners surrender to God and each other. This relationship is not centred on "me and my" but on "us and our". This is one secret to a lasting marriage and honouring before God.

1.3 Why Is living Together Before Marriage Considered living In Sin?

- When we refer to living together, we are referring to living together in the sense of living as husband and wife, including sexual relations, without being married. We are not referring to a man and woman living in the same house without sexual relations.
- Any sexuality outside of marriage of one man and one woman is definitely sin. There are numerous scriptures that declare God's prohibition of sexual immorality (Acts 15:20; 1 Corinthians 5:1; 6:13, 18; 10:8, 2 Corinthians 12:21; Galatians 5:19; Ephesians 5:3; Colossians 3:5; 1 Thessalonians 4:3; Jude 7).
- The only form of lawful sexuality is the marriage of one man and one woman (Genesis 2:24; Matthew 19:5), and anything outside marriage, whether it is adultery, premarital sex, homosexuality, or anything else, is unlawful: in other words, sin.
- Living together before marriage definitely falls into the category of fornication—sexual sin.

- The book of *Hebrews 13:4* describes the honourable state of marriage: "Marriage should be honoured by all, and the marriage bed kept pure, for God will judge the adulterer and all the sexually immoral."
- Anyone living together outside of lawful marriage invites the displeasure and judgment of God.

1.4 How Can Married Christians Avoid Emotional Affairs?

- An emotional affair occurs when a married person shares emotional intimacy with an individual others than his or her spouse. Marital partners should share problems, feelings and needs with one another and determine the boundaries of what can be shared and to whom. Depending on others to meet our emotional needs can become a temptation, especially when spouses spend much time apart while spending large blocks of time of time with others. Work relationships and friendships need to have proper boundaries to ensure they do not become inappropriate.
- The warning signs that a platonic friendship could be leading to an emotional affair: a. When we start to feel a need to hide aspects of a relationship, then we are crossing the line into inappropriate territory. b. Emotional distance between spouses or an increase in arguments may indicate that one spouse is turning to another person for closeness. c. Intimacy requires closeness and that cannot happen if a spouse gives his or her closeness to someone outside marriage. d. Emotional affairs often lead to sexual affairs as the intimate

emotional closeness shifts to physical closeness. Many people deny the seriousness of an emotional affair, but such an affair is not harmless and can destroy marriages and families.

- Christians should make choices that guard against the temptation to lean on someone other than the spouse God has given to them. Some area. Do not spend time alone with anyone of the opposite gender, especially someone you are attracted to. b. Do not spend more time with another person than with your spouse. c. Do not share intimate details of life with anyone before sharing them with your spouse. d. Live transparently. Do everything as if your spouse is present. e. Devote personal time to prayer and Bible study. Ask God to put a hedge around your marriage. f. Maintain a pure thought life. Do not entertain fantasies about other people. g. Plan time with your spouse on a daily, weekly and monthly basis and use those times to build emotional closeness between you.
- All these choices will help Christians to identify weak areas and avoid the temptations of an emotional affair.
- Christian priorities must put marriage and family second only to the Lord. As the Lord designed marriage to make two people into one person (Genesis 2:24), He wants them to grow together and let nothing separate them (Matthew 19:6).
- Married partners must value their relationship in the way the Lord values marriage and work on ways to build closeness in order to strengthen it.

- The Lord also forbids adultery or lusting for a person outside of marriage (Proverbs 6:25; Exodus 20:14; Matthew 5:28).
- People who go outside the Lord's design to meet their needs will ultimately sin against God and potentially ruin their relationship with Him and with one another (Proverbs 6:32; 1 Corinthians 6:19-20). God intended for married people to share a life together and create a family.
- Those who do not understand God's plan for married people can be misled into thinking it is unhealthy to share everything with one person, but that is what makes it different to any other relationship.
- Marriage is a blessed union between two people and mirrors that of Christ and His church.

2. *Youth and Single Adults*

2.1 Christian Relationship Advice
- Be more concerned with your relationship with God.
- Speak with God about your relationship a. Pray to God, asking Him to clearly reveal to you what He would want you to do (Philippians 4:6-7). b. Ask God to give you wisdom and discernment (James 1:5). God promises to grant prayer requests that are asked according to His will (1 John 5:14-15). Being wise and discerning are most definitely God's will.
- God wants you to make good relationship decisions
- God wants Christians to be happy and edified as a result of their relationships. If you ask God with an

open heart and humble spirit, He will give you the relationship advice you need.
- Lastly, find wise counsel with mature Christians who have been married for many years and have walked with God all that time.

2.2 Youth Ministry
- Youth Ministry is a permanent structure in churches today.
- Every ministry's goal is to make disciples.
- Student ministry should be purposeful, active, engaging and spiritually biblical. It needs to follow the model (2 Timothy 3:16-17). The leaders (i.e. adults, mentors, pastors, youth leaders) are there to mentor and equip these young ministers in Christ—like character, sound doctrine, and effective methods to reach lost peers and make disciples of their own (Matthew 28:18-20).
- The goal of having Youth Ministry is to make disciples and seeing the power of God unleashed in and through the lives of young people.
- Youth are at the point in their lives where they need to know the truth of God, how to live a life pleasing to Him, and what task He has called them to. As long as our motivation and message match that of Christ, then our ministries to youth are not only biblical, but necessary.

2.3 What Is True Friendship?
- Jesus is the pure example of a true friend, for He laid down His life for His "friends". What is more, anyone may became His friend by trusting in Him

as his personal saviour, being born again and receiving new life in Him (John 15:13-15).

- An example of true friendship is that between David and Saul's son Jonathan (1 Samuel 18:1-4; 19:4-7; 20:11-17; 41-42).
- Proverbs is another good source of wisdom regarding friends (Proverbs 17:17; 18:24; 27:6; 27:17).
- The principle of friendship is also found in *Amos 3:3*: "Friends are of like minds".
- Friendship is a relationship that is entered into by individuals, and it is only as good or as close as those individuals choose to make it.
- A friend is someone in whom you can confide with complete trust.
- A friend is someone you respect and who also respects you, not based upon worthiness but based upon a likeness of mind (Romans 5:7-8; John 15:13). Now that is true friendship.

2.4 Why Is Sexual Purity So Important?

- God gave man and woman the joy and pleasure of sexual relations within the bounds of marriage. The Bible is clear about the importance of maintaining sexual purity within the boundaries of that union between man and wife (Ephesians 5:31).
- What God says about purity is: "You should be sanctified, that you should avoid sexual immorality, that each of you should learn to control his own body in a way that is holy and honourable, not in passionate lust like the heathen, who do not know God. For God did not call us to be impure, but to live a holy life" (1 Thessalonians 4:3-5, 7).

- Being "sanctified" means literally "purified", made holy, consecrated (unto God). As Christians we have to live a purified life because we have been made holy by exchange of our sin for the righteousness of Christ on the cross and been made a completely new creations in Christ (2 Corinthians 5:17-21) Our old natures, with all their impurities, sexual and otherwise, have died and now the life we live we live by faith in the one who died for us (Galatians 2:20).
- The book of 1 Thessalonians 4:3-5 tells us about the necessity of controlling our bodies. When we give in to sexual immorality, we give evidence that the Holy Spirit is not indwelling in us because we do not posses one of the fruits of spirit—self-control (Galatians 5:22-23; 5:19) By controlling ourselves we honour with our bodies (1 Corinthians 6:18-20).
- By maintaining sexual purity before marriage, we avoid past emotionally difficult relationship that may negatively affect present relationships and marriages. By keeping the marriage bed pure (Hebrews 13:4), we can experience unreserved love for our mates, which is surpassed only by God's enormous love for us.

2.5 How Can I Know That I am In Love?
- Love is a very powerful emotion. It motivates most of our lives. We make many important decisions based on this emotion, and even get married because we feel that we are "in love". This may be the reason about half of all first marriages end up in divorce. The Bible teaches us that true love is not an emotion that can come or go, but a

decision. We are not just to love those who love us; we should even love those who hate us, the same way that Christ loves the unlovable (Luke 6:35). "Love is patient, love is kind. It does not envy, it does not boast, it is not proud. It is not rude, it is not self-seeking, it is not easily angered, and it keeps no record of wrongs. Love does not delight in evil but rejoices with the truth. It always protects, always trusts, always hopes, always perseveres" (1 Corinthians 13:4-7).

- It can be very easy to "fall in love" with someone, but there are some questions to ask before deciding if what we are feeling is true love

  a. Is this person a Christian, meaning have they given their life to Christ?
  b. Is he or she trusting Christ alone for salvation?
  c. If you are considering giving your heart and emotions to one person, you should ask yourself if you are willing to put that person above all other people and put your relationship second only to God. The Bible tells us that when two people get married, they become one flesh (Genesis 2:24; Matthew 19:5).
  d. Consider whether or not the loved one is a good candidate for being a mate. Has he or she already put God first and foremost in his or her life? e. Are they able to give time and energy to building the relationship into a marriage that will last a life time?

- There is no measuring stick to determine when we are truly in love with someone, but it is important to find out whether we are following our emotions or following God's will for our lives. True love is a decision, not just an emotion.

- *True Biblical love loves someone all the time, not just when you feel "in love".*

2.6 Why is Premarital Counselling Important?

- Premarital counselling usually falls under the office of the pastor or leader of a local church or congregation. In some congregations, the pastor will not undertake to perform a marriage ceremony unless the engaged couple submits to a series of counselling sessions. Pastors are concerned that those that are joined in marriage have the best chance of remaining "married". They see premarital counselling as an important part of getting a young couple off on the right track.
- The book of *Titus 2:1-6* shows us the type of counselling which has at its core the idea of teaching biblical truths, standards or absolutes in one's relationship to others.
- It is therefore important that the couple who intends to form a union making them one in God's eyes (Genesis 2:23-24; Mark 10: 6-8) be instructed in God's viewpoint concerning marriage.
- Premarital counselling, based upon sound biblical principles, outlines the role of the husband and wife as they relate to each other and to their prospective children (Ephesians 5:22-6:4; Colossians 3:18-21).
- Pastoral counselling should be in addition to the nurturing and godly wisdom the couple has (hopefully) received from their own parents.

- Parents are responsible before God to prepare children for adulthood, and that includes marriage.
- Premarital counselling is an excellent way to clear up the misconception about the roles we are to play in marriage and distinguish between God's standards and those of the world.
- It is crucial that the pastor or elder doing the premarital counselling be doctrinally solid, secure in his own marriage and family relationship (1 Timothy 3:4-5; Titus 1:7), and in obedience to God's Word so that he is equipped to impart God's viewpoint clearly and without equivocation (without making unclear statements).
- Solid, biblical premarital counselling may very well be the difference between a couple that seeks to put God's principles first in their marriage and a marriage based on human viewpoints and worldly standards that put the relationship in jeopardy.
- Serious consideration on the part of the prospective bride and groom to commit to a time of spiritual premarital counseling—and their agreement to model their marriage after God's order—will bring clarity to how each one views the other one in their "oneness" in the eyes of God.

2.7 Preventing Our Young People From Losing Faith
- Large numbers of today's youth are disenchanted with the church.
- Our youth need to fully understand that scripture alone can give life and bring sanctification to a sinful soul, and only scripture can equip us to

discern truth from lies and wrongdoing (Romans 10:14).

- In a world in which there is a growing tide of hostility towards Christianity, we need to teach our children the Word of God and how to defend it (1 Peter 3:15).
- Children must learn and develop their world view and belief systems in school, church and home.
- AT THE CHURCH—This is certainly a place where the truth of God's Word should be vigorously defended.
- AT HOME—Is where the development of Christian foundation starts with the parents.

a. Children are a gift from God (Psalm 127:3).

b. Parental influence in their children's lives is significant, and it is our responsibility as parents to pass along our faith and values to them.

c. In the Old Testament, Moses stressed to his people the importance of teaching children about the LORD and HIS commandments, decrees and Laws (Deuteronomy 11:19-20).

d. In the New Testament, parents are taught to raise their children in "the training and instruction of the Lord" (Ephesians 6:4), as all scripture is God-breathed and is useful for teaching, training and correcting (2 Timothy 3:16). Parents need to instil in their children a thoroughly Christian world vision so that they understand that the only way to God is through Jesus Christ (John 14:6). This requires studying the Bible and a lot of the Lord's work. For our children to be able to defend the Word of God (1 Peter 3:15), they need to know it well.

- Jesus Christ said in Matthew 7:24-25 that it is important that we construct a Christian life in our children's hearts at a tender age.

G Why Do So Many People Seek After Signs And Wonders?

Yes, our God is the God of wonders (Psalm 136:3-4). As the Creator and sustainer of all that is, God has the power to suspend natural laws in order to fulfil his purposes. Miracles were a part of the ministries of Moses, Elijah and Elisha, And, of course, Jesus and the Apostles, and their miracles, primarily served the purpose of confirming their message as being from God (Hebrews 2:3-4). Today, many people still seek to experience the miraculous, and some will go to great lengths to have that experience. There may be many reasons for such a desire, and scripture gives us at least five reasons:

1. **Some people seek after signs and wonders because they want confirmation of the truth of God.**

    - There is nothing inherently wrong with this desire. In fact, God willingly gave signs to Moses (Exodus 4:1-9) and Gideon (Judges 6:11-22) to confirm His word. Miracles can make a person come to faith, as in *John 2:23*, "Many people saw the miraculous signs he was doing and believed in his name."
    - However, there comes a time when enough miracles have been performed—the truth has been proved—and it is time to exercise faith. When

Moses hesitated to obey after a series of miracles at the burning bush, "the Lord's anger burned" (Exodus 4:14).

- Also, it is nobler in God's sight to believe *without* needing a miracle. Jesus visited the Samaritans, and "because of His words many more became believers" (John 4:41). Just a few verses later, Jesus rebukes the Galileans: "Unless you people see miraculous signs and wonders . . . you will never believe" (John 4:48). Unlike Samaritans, the people of Galilee required signs and wonders.

2. Some people seek after signs and wonder because they do not believe the signs and wonders which have already been performed

- For example, the Pharisees of Matthew 12 were just such a lot (Matthew 12:38-39; Exodus 9:34-35).

3. Some people seek after signs and wonders because they seek an occasion to excuse their unbelief.

- There were people in Jesus' day who "tested" Him by seeking a sign (Matthew 16:1; Luke 11:16). Since they specified that the sign be "from heaven", they most likely wanted something spectacular, similar to Elijah's calling down fire from the sky (1 Kings 18:38) or Isaiah's causing the sun to reverse course (Isaiah 38:8). Probably, their "test" was designed to be something "too big" for Jesus to accomplish—they simply hoped He would attempt it and fail.

4. **Some people seek after signs and wonders because they are curious thrill-seekers.**

    - Like the crowds in *John 6:2* and King Herod in *Luke 23:8,* they want to see something sensational, but they have no real desire to know the truth of Christ.

5. **Some People seek after signs and wonders because they hope to get something for themselves.**

    - After Jesus fed the multitudes, a large crowd followed Him to the other side of Galilee. Jesus saw their true motivation, however, and rebuked it (John 6:26). The crowd's desire was not to know Christ or even to see more miracles; it was simply to fill their stomachs again.

Better than seeking after a new miracle is taking God at His Word.

Simple faith is more pleasing to the Lord than a reliance on a dazzling sensory experience. "Jesus told him, 'Because you have seen me, you have believed; blessed are those who have not seen and yet have believed'" (John 20:29).

H

What Does The Bible Say About Ancestor Worship?

1. The Bible tells us that the spirit of the dead go to either heaven or hell and do not remain in the natural world (Luke 16:20-31; 2 Corinthian 5:6-10; Hebrews 9: 27; Revelation 20:11-15). The belief that spirits continue to reside on earth after death and influence the lives of others is not scriptural.

2. Nowhere in the Bible are we told that the dead act as intermediaries between God and man, but we are told that Jesus Christ was given that role. He was born, lived a sinless life, was crucified for our sins, buried in the grave, resurrected by God, seen by a multitude of witnesses, ascended into heaven, and sits now at the right hand of the Father where He intercedes on the behalf of those who have placed their faith and trust in Him (Acts 26:23; Romans 1:2-5; Hebrews 4:15; 1 Peter 1:3-4).

There is only one mediator between God and man and that is God's son, Jesus Christ (1 Timothy 2:5-6; Hebrews 8:6; 9:15; 12:24). Only Christ can fill that role.

- The Bible tells us in *Exodus 20: 3-6* that we are not to worship any god other than the Lord God. Furthermore, since diviners and sorcerers who were thought to be able to contact the dead were also expressly forbidden by God from doing so (Exodus 22:18; Leviticus 19:32, 20:6;27; Deuteronomy 18:10-11; 1 Samuel 28:3; Jeremiah 27:9-10).

- Satan has always sought to supplant God, and he uses lies about worshipping other gods and even ancestors to try and lead people away from the truth of God's existence. Ancestor worship is wrong because it goes against God's specific warnings about such worship, and it seeks to replace Jesus Christ as the divine mediator between God and mankind.

12 Ways to Develop a Positive Attitude

1. **BECOME AN AMBASSADOR OF GOOD WORKS TO EVERY PERSON YOU MEET EVERY DAY:**
    Wherever you are, be it at work or home, be friendly and be welcoming to everybody, whether young or old, rich or poor.

2. **NO MATTER WHAT HAPPENS, LOOK FOR THE GOOD AND YOU WILL FIND IT:**
    Positive thinking is the form of thought which habitually looks for the best results from the worst conditions. The fact is that when you seek good you will find it. Don't always look on the wrong or negative side when judging a person or situation.

3. **BY AN ACT OF YOUR WILL, FILL YOUR MIND WITH WHAT IS POSITIVE**
    Fix your thoughts on what is true and good and right. In everything, give thanks, even if you are suffering, you are treated unfairly, you are misunderstood or you are taken advantage of, whether things go well or go wrong (Ephesians 5:20, 1Thessalonians 5:18).

4. **NEVER SURRENDER TO NEGATIVE EMOTIONS**
    The way to destroy a negative emotion is to verbalize a positive statement by confessing good out of a bad

situation. For example, you could say I am rich while you don't have anything in your pocket.

5. **PRACTISE THE PRINCIPLE OF REPLACEMENT**
Always replace bad with good, for example anger with love, fear with faith, despair with hope, greed with generosity, sorrow with joy, complaint with gratitude, worry with trust and guilt with forgiveness.

6. **BAR THE SUGGESTIVE, THE LEWD, THE PERVERTED, THE IMMORAL. AND THE VULGAR FROM YOUR MIND**
You cannot feed on garbage and stay healthy and sound in mind (Romans 12:2). You keep your mind healthy by living in fellowship with God. If you put *garbage into your mind—you're going to get garbage out. Put good thoughts into your mind and good actions will come out.*

7. **SEE GOOD IN OTHERS**
Let's stop creating a negative atmosphere wherever we go, talking about everything and everyone in a negative way. Every time you talk negatively about another human being, you infect the atmosphere with bad feeling. Look for the good in everybody you meet and you will find it.

8. **BE DETERMINED TO TAKE AN ATTITUDE OF LOVE AND GOODWILL TOWARD OTHERS**
Change your attitude towards other people and other people will change their attitude towards you. Your attitude towards the people who are around

you is always bound to transmit and communicate itself. Love people and they will love you back.

9. **EXPRESS APPRECIATION AND WARM FEELING TO OTHERS**
Express gratitude or words of appreciation, or show love for another person.

10. **PRACTISE POSITIVE PRAYER:**
Nothing clears the mind like prayer. Whatever you ask and pray for, if you believe that you will receive it, you shall have it. (Mark 11:23, Romans 8:31, Isaiah 40:31, Matthew 9:29, Philippians 4:13).

11. **YOU CAN COUNT ON IT: GOD IS GOOD, AND HE HAS A PLAN FOR YOUR LIFE**
He will not fail you. He will not let you down. He will bring good out of bad.
Plan something big! Get an exciting idea and put it into action.

12. **EXPECT THE BEST—AND YOU WILL GET IT**
Jesus Christ is the great transformer. Keep on keeping on. It takes not just one choice or two or three, but thousands of choices to become a positive-thinking person. Old habits do not die easily. New habits do not die easily. New habits are established by great effort and persistence.

BELIEVE THE BEST IS YET TO COME

If you believe, there is no situation you cannot overcome:
   You can overcome illness, you can overcome weakness, you can overcome sin, you can overcome heartbreak, you can overcome failure

BELIEF IS:

The magic that lights up ones life with possibilities.
The initiator of all achievement.
The hook-up to a power greater than we are.
Jesus believes you are a dream that can come true.
God believes in you, now believe in yourself.

All things are possible if you believe in God.
They conquer who believe they can
Faith in God can move a mighty mountain

NEVER STOP BELIEVING

J

Enjoy your freedom

Personal Evaluation

This teaching clarifies a lot of things about freedom and how you can enjoy it.

He states that when you are free in Christ, only then you will be free from law, sin, men and your past.

WHAT IS FREEDOM?

- Freedom is the privilege and power to become all that God wants you to become.
- Freedom is the opportunity to fulfil your potential to the glory of God.

To understand and enjoy freedom, you must understand the three affirmations that the Lord Jesus has made:

1. God's purpose for man is freedom
2. God's method for freedom is truth
3. God's revelation of truth is Jesus Christ

1. God's Purpose for Man

God's purpose for man is Freedom.

When you were born again through faith in Jesus Christ, God added spiritual gifts to your natural talents. God surrounds you with opportunity. Freedom is the opportunity to fulfil your potential to the glory of God.

2. God's Method for Freedom

God's methods for freedom is TRUTH. The Power of God works through truth and the power of the devil works through lies. Satan is the liar (John 8:44). Jesus is the truth . . . (John 14:6). The word of God is truth (John 17:17, John 8:31, 32).

3. God's Revelation of Truth

God's revelation of truth is Jesus Christ (John 8:36). The better you know the Lord Jesus Christ, the more freedom you are going to enjoy.

FALSE FREEDOM

Christian Freedom is a life controlled by TRUTH and motivated by LOVE.

It is the result of a growing relationship with Jesus Christ, who is the Truth, and with the word of God, and with the Holy Spirit of God, who is the spirit of truth. But there is a FALSE freedom in the world today, a freedom that comes not from heaven but from hell. Those who practise this false freedom have a life that is controlled by lies and motivated by lust (2 Peter 2:1-3).

Where False Freedom Comes From

It comes from false teachers. There were false prophets among Israel, and there are going to be false teachers among Christians today. These teachers claim to believe in the Lord and to follow the word of God, and yet they so twist the Word of God and so misapply the Word of God that they lead people into bondage (2 Peter 2:10).

What False Freedom Offers

1. Freedom without responsibility: Whatever gives you freedom without your self-control will lead you into bondage and destruction. The Prodigal son wanted freedom, but he did not want responsibility. Unearned freedom is a dangerous, destructive thing (Genesis 3:1, 4,5).
2. Freedom without reckoning: They say there will not be any judgment. Sometimes they even use the Bible to teach their false doctrines (Romans 6:1, 2).
3. Freedom without repercussions: They say you can go out and do that, and there won't be any consequences, you'll get away with it! But you can't get away with it: "the wages of sin is death" (Romans 6:23).
4. Freedom without recession: Sin begins with a great deal of pleasure and ends with pain. Sin enslaves those who practise it.

Where False Freedom Leads

It leads to bondage and judgment (2 Peter 2:19).

FREEDOM FROM LAW

1) Law as a guardian: As little children we need guardians because we are immature and lack the discernment of adults (Galatians 4:6, 7). Christ has redeemed us from the law and we now have a position in the family as adult sons.

2) Law as a slave girl: Sarah was a freewoman, but Hagar was a slave. Sarah represents the heavenly Jerusalem, but Hagar represents the earthly Jerusalem in bondage (Genesis 16 and Galatians 4:21-31).

3) Law as a bond of indebtedness: You and I had a bond of indebtedness that we could not pay. We were totally bankrupt. When Jesus died for us on the cross, He not only washed away the writing on the document but He also nailed the document to His cross (Ephesians 2:14, Galatians 6:14).

4) Law as a shadow: Heavenly, spiritual realities are pictured in earthly, physical copies. The tabernacle was a copy of God's tabernacle in heaven. When you put yourself under the law, you are exchanging the reality for the copy.

5) Law as a mirror: The law is a mirror that reveals sin. The law is God's mirror to show us how dirty we are. When I read the word of God, I realize that I am a sinner and therefore need a saviour (James 1:22-25).

6) Law as a husband: When you have been saved through Jesus Christ, you are united to Him in His death, burial and resurrection. That means you are married, not to the law but to Jesus Christ. Your relationship is one of love and life, not one of law (Romans 7:1-4).

FREEDOM FROM SIN

Every Christian has to battle with three enemies: The world, the flesh and the devil (Ephesians 2:1-3). Before you become a Christian, you live according to the dictates of this world. You are controlled by the power of Satan, and live to satisfy the desires of the flesh. When you become a Christian, you are set free from these enemies, but they are still enemies! Through Jesus Christ, we can have freedom from the sins of the flesh. In *Romans 6* we are told how to live in victory over the flesh.

We should KNOW, RECKON and YIELD.
He gave instruction to the mind: KNOW
He gave instruction to the heart: RECKON
HE gave instruction to the will: YIELD

FREEDOM FROM MEN

For he that is called, is free, is Christ's servant (1 Corinthians 7:17-24).

Freedom from people is in three different aspects:

The setting: The freedom in Jesus Christ must not be abused and turned into license.

The meaning:
  i   We are called by God
  ii   We have been assigned by God
  iii We belong to God iv We should abide with God

The Application: How can we practically apply this truth in our lives? Don't live in fear of other people (Proverbs 29:25). You must care about, but not be enslaved to, the opinions of others.

FREEDOM FROM THE PAST

We cannot change the past, but we can be changed by the past. Many people are controlled by past sins, past regrets and past failures. The past should be there to guide us and not to drag us back (1 Timothy 1:12-17).

Accept God's Forgiveness:

If you are a Christian, God has completely dealt with all your sin and you are justified (Colossians 1:14; 2:13, Genesis 50, Micah 7:19, Isaiah 38:17, Hebrews 10:17, Psalms 103:12).

Forgive Others:

One evidence of true repentance is that we can forgive others. "If you forgive men their trespasses, your heavenly Father will also forgive you" (Matthew 6:11, 14).

Forgive Yourself

People do not forgive themselves because of pride. When you think of the past, turn it into prayer and praise (1 Timothy 1:17, Psalms 103:14).

FREEDOM FROM THINGS

Christians of today need to be delivered from things they don't admit that they worry about. They called it being "burdened" or being "concerned", but worry is what it really is (Matthew 6:19-34).

It is not wrong to own things: Genesis 1:31

i God made things that are good.

ii God knows that we need things (Matthew 6:32).

iii God wants us to enjoy and use things (1 Timothy 6:17).

It is wrong for things to own us:

Things are marvellous servants but terrible masters (Matthew 6:21).

God must be the master: Matthew 6:33

When God is first and we are worshiping Him and not things, then people and things fall into their proper place.

FUTURE FREEDOM

Christians enjoy freedom now, but our greatest experience of freedom will take place in the future, when Jesus returns: the glorious liberty of the children of God (Romans 8:18-23).

Contrast between suffering and glory

Today we are experiencing suffering, but in that future liberty of the children of God, there will be glory (2 Corinthians 4:16-18).

Contrast between expectation and manifestation

All creation is waiting for the sons of God to be manifested (Romans 8:19, Romans 8:21, 1 John 3:2, John 17:24).

Contrast between vanity and hope

We have a living hope. Today the world is subjected to vanity, but when Jesus returns, we will experience the fulfilment of this blessed hope, "the glorious liberty of the children of God" (Romans 8:20-21).

Contrast between bondage and liberty

The creation itself also shall be delivered from the bondage of corruption into the glorious liberty of the children of God. The contrast is between the bondage of corruption and the liberty of God's children.

Contrast between groaning and redemption

We are groaning within ourselves, waiting for Jesus to come. We are groaning for glory. All the vanity of life will one day be replaced by the fulfilment of hope. The bondage of corruption will be replaced by the glorious liberty of the children of God. The groaning will be replaced by the adoption, the redemption of our bodies (Romans 8:22, 23).

K "Pray What the Word of God Says"

Putting God First

But seek first the kingdom of God and his righteousness, and all things shall be added to you (Matthew 6:33).

Father, your word says that if any man be in Christ, he is a new creature: old things are passed away; behold, all things are become new. I thank you Jesus Christ that my life has been redeemed and I am your servant who walks in newness. I put you first and foremost in all things concerning my life because I have been bought with the price by your precious blood. I am a member of your body, of your flesh and bones. I abide in you, my Lord and God, by the Holy Spirit. I keep my ears open to hear and obey your voice, to observe and to do all that you have commanded by your word. I do not refuse to hear or receive instruction and wisdom and I incline my ears to hear your voice. Daily I am watchful and wait upon you for the wisdom of your counsel of truth and I know that I shall always be blessed when I reverence and honour you, Lord.

In Jesus' Name I pray, Amen

"THANDAZA LOKO UTHIXO AKUSHOYO"

U Jehovah makabe sisiqalo empilweni

Funa kuqala ubukumkani buka Jehovah, noku lunga kwakhe, ukuze zonke izinto zengezelelwe empilweni yakho (Matewu 6:33).

Baba izwi lakho lithi ukuba umntu uku Krestu, usisidalwa esitsha: zonke izinto ezindala zidlulile konke kutsha kuye. Ndiyakubonga Yesu Kristu ngokuba ubomi bam butshintshile ndingumthunywa wakho ozelwe kabutsha. Ndikwenza owokuqala kubomi bam bonke ngokuba ndithengwe ngegazi lakho elinqabileyo. Ndili lungu lomzimba wakho inyama namathambo akho. Ndiyazinikela kuwe Jehovah Thixo wam, ngoMoya oYingcwele. Ndihlala ndizivulile iindlebe zam ukuva nokuthobela izwi lakho, ukwenza konke endiku yalelwa yizwi lakho. Andali ukuthatha nokumamela imiyalelo nentlakanipho ndihlale enyanisweni kwaye ndiyazi ndohlala ndibusisiwe xa ndihlonipha wena Nkosi.

Sikucela konke oku egameni lika Jesu Kristu Amen

Scriptures for Putting God First

Matthew 6:33—But seek first the kingdom of God and his righteousness, and all things shall be added to you.

1 Corinthians 7:20-24—Let each one remain in the same calling in which he was called. Were you called while a slave? Do not be concerned about it; but you can be made free, rather use it. For he who was called in the Lord while a slave is the Lords freedman. Likewise he who is called while free is Christ's slave. You were bought at a price; do not become a slave of men.

Brethren, let each one remain with God in that state in which he was called

2 Corinthians 5:17—Therefore if anyone is in Christ, he is a new creation; old things have passed away; behold, all things have become new.

Deuteronomy 28:1—Now it shall come to pass, if you diligently obey the voice of the Lord your God, to observe carefully all

His commandments which I command you today, that the Lord your God will set you high above all nations of the earth.

Ephesians 5:30—For we are members of His body, of his flesh and of His bones.

Genesis 12:3—I will bless those who bless you, and I will curse him who curses you; and in you all the families of the earth shall be blessed.

Proverbs 8:33-36—Hear instruction and be wise, and do not disdain it. Blessed is the man who listens to me, watching daily at my gates, Waiting at the post of my doors, for whoever finds me finds life, and obtains favour from the Lord. But he who sins against me, wrongs his own soul; all those who hate me love death.

Psalm 128:4—Behold, thus shall the man be blessed who fears the Lord.

PRAYER FOR DELIVERANCE

"Call to me, and I will answer you, and show you great and mighty things, which you do not know" (Jeremiah 33:3).

Thank you, Lord, for your word that says that no weapon formed against me shall prosper. This is my heritage because I am a servant of the Lord and my righteousness is of God. In your righteousness, Lord, I am established and kept far from oppression. I do not fear and terror does not come near me. My ears are attentive to hear your word behind me, giving me direction and instruction in the way that I shall walk. When you say this is the way, I will walk in it whether it is to the left or the right. When I call upon the name of the Lord, I am delivered, even if I am counted and called among the remnant. I trust in you Lord with all my heart. I lean not on my understanding and in all my ways I acknowledge you and you direct my paths. My paths are the shining light that shine more and more unto the perfect day.

The counsel, wisdom, understanding and strength of the Lord are mine. I am delivered out of trouble and the wicked are stopped. My steps take the way that is perfect because the word of the Lord has been tried in my life. Lord you are my buckler because I trust in you. Lord you are my hiding place and you preserve me from trouble. You encompass me about with songs of deliverance and instruct me and teach me in the way that I shall go and you are steadily guiding me with your eye. With you is the fountain of life and in your light I see light. Father, continue to send out your light and your truth so that it will lead me and bring me into your holy presence and dwelling places.

In Jesus' Name I Pray. Amen.

UMTHANDAZO WOKU HLANGULWA

"Biza kum ndiya kukuphendula, Ndikibonise izinto ezinkulu nezimangalisayo, ongazaziyo" (Yeremiya 33:3)

Ndiyabulela Nkosi, ngelizwi elithi asikho isikhali esibekelwe thina esingaphumelela, nalo naliphi Na ilwimi elithetha kakubi ngam ndinokuligxeka. Lilo Ixesha lam Eli, ngokuba ndisisicaka sakho nokulunga kwam kokuka Jehova. Ngoku lunga kwakho ndisindisiwe ndakhutshwa kwingcindezelo. Andoyiki, akukho nto yothusayo isondelayo kum. Iindlebe zam ndizibazele ukumamela ilizwi elivakla emva kwam, elindikhombisa indlela emandihambe ngayo. Ndiza kulandela yona, nokuba uthi mandiye ngasekunxele okanye ekunene. Xa ndibiza igama lika Yehova, ndiya kuhlanguleka nokuba sebalelwe kwaba boshiweyo ... Ndikuthemba ngentliziyo yam yonke.

Andimi ekwazini nakwiindlela zam, ndiyazi uyandibonisa iindlela zam. Iindlela zam zikukukhanya okukhanya yonke imihla.

Iingcebiso, intlakanipho, ukuqonda kukaJehiova kokwam. Ndihlanguliwe ezingxakini noku khohlakala kuphelile. Iihambo zam zihamba indlela eyiyo ngokuba izwi lenkosi liyasebenza empilweni yam. Yehova usisiqhoboshi sam ndiya kwethemba. Yehova usisiphephelo sam uyandifihla ezingxakini. Undingqonga ngeengoma zondihlangula undixelele undifundise ngendlela emandihambe ngayo uhlala undigadile ngelihlo lakho. Xa ndinawe ndinomthombo wobomi ekukhanyeni kwakho ndibona ukukhanya. Bawo qhubeka uthumele ukhanyo lwakho nenyaniso yakho ukuze indikhokhele indizise ebungcwaliseni nakwi ndawo zakho zokuhlala.

Ngegama lika Jesu Kristu siyathandaza ... Amen!!

SCRIPTURES FOR DELIVERANCE

Jeremiah 33:3—'Call to me, and I will answer you, and show you great and mighty things, which you do not know'

Isaiah 30:21—And thy ears shall hear a word behind thee, saying, This is the way, walk ye in it, when ye turn to the right hand, and when ye turn to the left.

Isaiah 54:17—No weapon that is formed against thee shall prosper; and every tongue that shall rise against thee in judgment thou shalt condemn. This is the heritage of the servants of the Lord, and their righteousness is of me, saith the Lord.

Isaiah 54:14—In righteousness shalt thou be established: thou shall be far from oppression; for thou shalt not fear: and from terror; for it shall not come near thee.

Joel 2:32—And it shall come to pass that whosoever shall call on the name of the Lord shall be delivered, for in mount Zion and in Jerusalem shall be deliverance, as the Lord hath said, and in the remnant whom the Lord shall call.

Proverbs 3:5-6—Trust in the Lord with all thy heart; and lean not unto thine own understanding. In all thy ways acknowledge him, and shall direct thy paths.

Proverbs 4:18—But the path of the just is as the shining light, that shineth more and more unto the perfect day.

Proverbs 8:14—Counsel is mine, and sound wisdom: I am understanding; I have strength.

Proverbs 11:8—The righteous is delivered out of trouble, and the wicked cometh in his stead.

Psalm 18:30—As for God, His way is perfect: the word of the Lord is tried: He is a buckler to all those that trust in him.

Psalm 32:7-8—Thou art my hiding place; thou shalt preserve me about with songs of deliverance. Selah. I will instruct thee and teach thee in the way which thou shalt go: I will guide thee and teach thee in the way which thou shalt go: I will guide thee with mine eye.

Psalm 36:9—For with thee is the fountain of life: in thy light shall see light.

Psalm 43:3—O send out thy light and thy truth: let them lead me; let them bring me unto thy holy hill, and to thy tabernacles.

PRAYER FOR INNER LIFE

Beloved, I pray that you prosper in all things and be in health, just as your soul prospers (3 John 1:2).

Father, I present my body as a living sacrifice, holy, acceptable unto you, which is my reasonable service. I am not to be conformed to this world, so I hold fast to the truth of your word that transforms and renews my mind. My lifestyle is the evidence that your word is working effectually in me. I am able to prove the good and acceptable and perfect will of God. May I be found a faithful steward over your word, steadfast, unmovable and always abounding in the work of the Lord? All of my labour, what I do in word or deed, is done in your name, Lord Jesus, so my labour is not in vain. Thank you for helping me to bear the burdens of others and to love others as you have loved me. I am counted in your eyes as one who, out of the good treasures of my heart, brings forth that which is good. Out of the abundance of my heart my mouth speaks the law of kindness, grace, comfort, edification and exhortation to others. My companions are those who are wise because destruction waits for those who walk with fools. When I rest I have your peace and sweet sleep and I dwell in the safety of your presence. My ears are attentive to your voice and you speak peace to your people and your saints and I am kept from turning again to folly. You are the God of patience and consolation and may I be like-minded toward others according to Christ Jesus. With one mind and one mouth I glorify God, even the Father of my Lord and saviour Jesus Christ. I receive others as Christ received me to the glory of God.

In Jesus' name I pray. Amen.

UMTHANDAZO WOMPHEFUMLO WAKHO.

Mhlobo oyintanda, ndithandazela ukuba kube hele, kube chosi kuwe, nanjengoko ndisazi ukuba kunjalo nasemphefumlweni wakho (3 John 1:2).

Bawo ndinikela ngomzimba wam, ugcwaliswe, wamkeleke kuwe, kuyiyo leyo injongo yam. Andinguye oweli hlabathi, kungoko ndibambelela enyanisweni yelizwi lakho eliguqulayo nelivuselela ingqondo yam. Indlela endiphila ngayo ibubungqina obubonisa ukuphila kwezwi lakho kum. Ndiyangqina ngoku lunga nokwa mkeleka kwentando ka Thixo. Mandibe ngothembekileyo ezwini lakho ndime ndinga gungqi ndizimisele ukwenza umsebenzi ka Thixo. Wonke umsebenzi wam, endiwenza ngokwe zwi okanye izenzo, kwenzeka egameni lenkosi uJesu, ngoko ke intsebenzo yam ayikho lize. Ndiyabulela ngokundinceda ukuba ndithwale imithwalo yabanye abantu ndibathande njengokuba nawe wandithanda. Ndibalwa emehlweni akho njengomnye olilungisa ngokwentliziyo nowenza okuhle. Ngokuvuya kwentliziyo, umlomo wam uthetha umthetho woku thobeka, ufefe, intuthuzelo, Nenqubela yabanye abantu. Ndihlanganyela nalabo abahlakaniphileyo kuba imbubhiso ilinde abo abahlangana nezibhanxa. Xa ndiphumlile ndiba noxolo nokulala okuhle kwaye ndikhuselekile xa ndinawe. Iindlebe zam zimamela izwi lakho kwaye uthetha uxolo kubantu bakho naku malungisa akho kwaye uyandikhusela ukuba ndingabuyeli kwindlela zonge ndawo. Ngomlomo nangengqondo yam ndiyakudumisa Thixo Ndikucela konke oku ngegama lika Jesu Kristu . . . . Amen!!

SCRIPTURES FOR THE INNER LIFE

3 John 1:2—Beloved, I pray that you may prosper in all things and be in health, just as your soul prospers.

1 Corinthians 4:2—Moreover it is required in stewards that one is found faithful.

1 Corinthians 15:58—Therefore, my beloved brethren, be steadfast, immovable, always abounding in the work of the Lord, knowing that your labour is not in vain in the Lord.

Colossians 3:17—and whatever you do in word or deed, do all in the name of the Lord Jesus, giving thanks to God the father through Him.

Galatians 6: 2—Bear one another's burdens, and so fulfil the law of Christ.

John 13:34—A new commandment I give to you, that you love one another; as I love you, that you also love one another.

Luke 6:45—A good man out of the good treasure of his heart brings forth well; and an evil man out of the evil treasure of his heart brings forth evil. For out of the abundance of the heart his mouth speaks.

Proverbs 13:20—He who walks with the wise men will be wise, but the companion of fools will be destroyed.

Psalm 4:8—I will both lie down in peace, and sleep; for you alone, O Lord, make me dwell in safety.

Psalm 85:8—I will hear what God the Lord will speak, For he speaks peace To His people and to His saints; But let them not turn back to folly.

Romans 12:1-2—I beseech you therefore, brethren, by the mercies of God, that you present your bodies a living sacrifice, holy, acceptable to God, which is your reasonable service. And do not be conformed to this world, but be transformed by the renewing of your mind, that you may prove what is that good and acceptable and perfect will of God.

Romans 15:5-7—Now may the God of patience and comfort grant you to be like-minded toward one another, according to Christ Jesus, that you may with one mind and one mouth glorify the God and Father of our Lord Jesus Christ.

PRAYER OF REST

"Come to me, all you who labour and are heavy laden, and I will give you rest" (Matthew 11:28).

Lord I find my rest in you and I wait patiently for you concerning all things pertaining to my life. I do not fret about others who prosper according to their own ways without your counsel, or those who bring wicked plans and devices to pass. When I am perplexed or dismayed, my soul will return into the dwelling place of your rest where I find your abundant peace. I resist every yoke and burden that is not of you, because your yoke is easy and your burden is light. You are able to save me from afar and deliver me from places of captivity so that I can be at rest, and be quiet and nothing causes me to be afraid.

In Jesus' name I pray. Amen!!

UMTHANDAZO WOKUPHUMLA KU JESU KRISTU

"Yizani kum Nina nonke enisindwayo, yimithwalo, ndiya kuninika ukuphumla" (Matewu 11:28).

Nkosi ndifumana ukuphumula kuwe ndikwa linde ngesizotha kuko konke okumalunga nobomi bam. Andoyikiswa ngabantu abaphumelela ngeendlela zabo ekungezizo ezakho, okanye abo abenza ububi benzeke. Xa ndikhathazekile ndiphoxekile umphefumlo wam uyabuyela kwindawo yokuphumla apho ndifumana uxolo olwaneleyo. Ndilwisana nako konke ukuhlupheka noku bandezelwa okunga veli kuwe, ngoba idyokhwe yakho ayikho nzima nomthwalo wakho ulula. Uyakwazi ukundisindisa ukude undihlangule kwindawo zababandezeli ukuze ndiphumle, ndibe nokuthula kungabikho nto endenza ndibe noloyiko.

Ngegama Lika Jesu Kristu Siyathandaza, Amen!!

SCRIPTURES FOR REST

Matthew 11:28—Come unto me, all ye that labour and are heavy laden, I will give you rest.

Jeremiah 30:10—Therefore fear thou not, O my servant Jacob, saith the Lord; neither be dismayed, O Israel: for, lo, I will save thee from afar, and thy seed from the land of their captivity; and Jacob shall return, and shall be in rest, and be quiet, and none shall make him afraid.

Matthew 11:29-30—Take my yoke upon you, and lean on me; for I am meek and lowly in heart: and ye shall find rest unto your souls. For my yoke is easy, and my burden is light.

Psalm 37:7—Rest in the Lord and wait for him: fret not thyself because of him who prospereth in his way, because of the man who bringeth wicked devices to pass.

Psalm 116: 7—Return unto thy rest, O my soul; for the Lord hath dealt bountifully with thee.

PRAYER OF RESTORATION

Restore to me the joy of my salvation, and uphold me by your generous Spirit (Psalm 51:12).

Thank you Lord for being the shepherd and restorer of my soul. You lead me in the sure paths of righteousness for your name's sake. My health is restored because every emotional, mental and physical wound is healed by your great and gracious power. The places that have been desolate and lay waste are rebuilt, every breach, gap and torn down hedge is repaired, my paths restored.

The foundation of your truth dwells richly and eternally in my heart, so I have nothing missing, broken or lacking in my life.

In Jesus' name I pray. Amen!!

UMTHANDAZO WOKUBUYISELWA ESIMWENI

Ndibuyisele uvuyo losindiso lwakho, undixhase ngomoya wakho, khon'ukuze ndikuthobele (Indumiso 51:12).

Ndiyakubulela Yehova ngokuba nguMalusi nombuyisi womphefumlo wam. Undikhokhelela ezindleleni zobulungisa ngenxa yegama lakho. Impilo yam ibuyisiwe ngenxa yemizwa, nengqondo kunye nezilonda zenyama zipholisiwe ngamandla amangalisayo. Iindawo ebezingamanxiwa zigcwele ukungcola zakhiwe ngabutsha, konke ukwahluleka, isithuba nothango oluwileyo lulungisiwe iindlela zibuyisiwe. Isisekelo senyaniso sohlala sityebileyo unaphakade entliziyweni yam, ngoko akukho nto ilahlekayo, ephukileyo okanye engagcwalisekanga ebomini bam.

Sikucela konke oku ngegama lika Jesu Kristu . . . Amen!!!

SCRIPTURES FOR RESTORATION

Psalm 51:12-13—Restore to me the joy of your salvation, and uphold me by your generous spirit. Then I will teach transgressors your ways, and sinners shall be converted to you.

Isaiah 58: 12—Those from among you shall build the old waste places; you shall rise up the foundations of many generations; and you shall be called the Repairer of the Breach, The restorer of the street to dwell in,

Jeremiah 30: 17—For I will restore health to you And heal you of your wounds, says the Lord, 'Because they called you an outcast saying: "This is Zion; No one seeks her."

Psalm 23: 3—He restores my soul; He leads me in the paths of righteousness for his name's sake

PRAYER OF MERCY

The lord is good! All the time!

God is faithful, He is full of compassion. His mercies are new every morning: great is your faithfulness (Lamentation 3:22-23).

Let us remind ourselves of the Benefits that are ours in JESUS as they are quoted in *Psalm 103*:

1. He forgives all our sins.
2. He heals all diseases.
3. He saves our lives from destruction.
4. He crowns us with loving kindness and tender mercies.
5. He satisfies our mouth with good things so that our youth is renewed like the Eagle.
6. He executes righteousness and judgment for us against oppression. He sets us free.
7. He makes known His way to us.

8. He gives us the grace and mercy in times of need, as in *Psalm 136*: "O give thanks unto the LORD, for he is good, for his mercy endures forever".

In *Exodus 33:18* Moses is asking GOD for Glory and GOD responded to Moses in *Exodus 34:6-7* . . . "And the LORD passed by before him and proclaimed the LORD, THE LORD GOD, MERCIFUL and GRACIOUS, LONG-SUFFERING, and ABUNDANT IN GOODNESS and TRUTH. Keeping mercy for thousands, forgiving iniquity of the fathers upon the children. And upon the children's children unto the third and fourth generation".

Pray after me . . . .

Father, I am standing before you as the prodigal son in Luke 15:21: "*Father, I have sinned against Heaven, and in your sight, and I am no more worthy to be called your son*".

Lord, I thank you for forgiving me and not even remembering my sins anymore. As it says in *Hebrews 8:12*: "*for I will be merciful to their unrighteousness*, and *their sins and their iniquities will I remember no more*". Show me anything I need to confess to you today so that I can bring it before you and be set free. Convict my heart any time I stray from your laws and commandments. Help me to be a forgiving person in the same way you are forgiving towards me. Lord, take away anything of anger or bitterness in my heart. Pour out your spirit upon me and cleanse me of all that is not of you. Enable me to be a person who lives in the forgiveness you have given me so that I can extend forgiveness freely toward others. As in *Ephesians 4:32: "And you be kind to one another, even as God for Christ's sake has forgiven you*".

PRAYER OF PRAISE

What is prayer? Prayer is simply communication with GOD.

The purest form of Prayer is praise and worship. It is pure because the focus is entirely on the LORD, not on US.

When we worship, we draw closer to GOD—just to be with him alone—and we communicate our reverence, love, thankfulness, devotion and praise to Him. When we open up our hearts to Him in praise, He pours Himself into us. He pours his love, peace, power, joy, goodness, wisdom, holiness, wholeness and freedom into us every time we worship him.

God created us to worship Him. It is what we are born to do (Psalm 150:6).

Psalm 103 says "BLESS THE LORD, O MY SOUL: AND ALL THAT IS WITHIN ME BLESS HIS HOLY NAME".

1. PRAISE STRENGTHENS AND TRANSFORMS YOUR SOUL: "In the day when I cried you answered. and strengthened me with the strength in my soul" (Psalms 138:1-3).
2. PRAISE TAKES AWAY FEAR: "I sought the LORD, and He heard me, and delivered me from all my fears" (Psalms 34:4).
3. PRAISE TAKES AWAY DOUBT: "The LORD is my light and my salvation, whom shall I fear? The LORD is the strength of my life. What shall I be afraid of? Wait on the LORD, be of good courage and he shall strengthen your heart; wait. I say on the LORD" (Psalm 27).

4. PRAISE RELEASES THE POWER OF GOD IN YOUR LIFE: "Blessed be the LORD my strength, who teaches my hands to war and my fingers to fight. Send your hand from above; rid me, and deliver me out of great waters, from the hand of foreigners" (Psalm 144).
5. PRAISE DESTROYS THE ENEMY'S PLANS: "When the wicked spring as the grass, and when all the workers of iniquity do flourish, it is that they shall be destroyed forevermore" (Psalm 92).

Pray after me . . .

Lord, I enter your gates with thanksgiving and your courts with praise. I worship you as the Almighty, all-powerful God of heaven and earth and the creator of all things. I praise you as my heavenly father, who is with me every day to guide and protect me. Thank you for all you have given me and all you will provide for me in the future. As you said in Psalm 16:5-6 . . . "You guard all that is mine; the land you have given me is a pleasant land". I praise you for your love that liberates me and makes me whole. Pour your love into me so that it overflows to others and glorifies you. Thank you for your greatest act of love by sending your son to die for me. I praise you, Jesus, my Lord and redeemer, for you have saved me, and given me a foundation that is unshakable. As is said in 2 Samuel 22:37, "You enlarged my path under me, so my feet did not slip".

It is my greatest privilege to exalt you above all and to proclaim that you are King of kings and Lord of lords. No one is greater than you.

I praise you for your Holy Spirit, who leads and comforts me.

I praise you for your peace and joy, I praise you for your wisdom and revelation.

Thank you that you are in charge of my life and nothing is too hard for you.

Thank you for enabling me to do what I could never do without you. Lord, help me to worship you in ways that are pleasing in your sight.

You are holy and worthy of all praise, and I exalt you above all things.

In Jesus' name I pray. Amen.

OPEN YOUR MOUTH AND PRAY . . . .

MEMORY VERSES

Isaiah 53:5-6—But He was wounded for our transgressions, He was bruised for our iniquities; the chastisement for our peace was upon Him, and by His stripes we are healed. All we are like sheep have gone astray; we have turned, every one, to his own way; and the Lord has laid on Him the iniquity of us all.

John 1:12—But as many as received Him, to them He gave the right to become children of God, to those who believe in His name:

John 3:16—For God so loved the world that He gave His only begotten Son, that whoever believes in Him should not perish but have everlasting life.

John 14:6—Jesus said to him, "I am the way, the truth, and the life. No one comes to the Father except through me.

1 John 5:13—These things I have written to you who believe in the name of the Son of God, that you may know that you have eternal life, and that you may continue to believe in the name of the son of God.

Acts 4:12—Nor is there salvation in any other, for there is no other name under heaven given among men by which we must be saved.

Acts 1:8—But you shall receive power when the Holy Spirit has come upon you; and you shall be witnesses to me in Jerusalem, and in all Judea and Samaria, and to the end of the earth.

Romans 1:16—For I am not ashamed of the Gospel of Christ for it is the power of God to Salvation for everyone who believes, for the Jews first and also for the Greek.

Romans 3: 23—For all have sinned and fall short of the Glory of God.

Romans 5:8—But God demonstrates His own love toward us, in that while we were still sinners, Christ died for us

Romans 6:23—For the wages of sin is death, but the gift of God is eternal life in Christ Jesus our Lord.

Romans 10:9—That if you confess with your mouth the Lord Jesus and believe in your heart that God has raised Him from the dead, you will be saved.

Ephesians 2:8-9—For by grace you have been saved through faith, and that not of yourselves; it is the gift of God, not of works, lest anyone should boast.

2 Corinthians 5:17—Therefore, if anyone is in Christ, he is a new creation; old things have passed away; behold, all things have become new.

Revelation 3:20—Behold, I stand at the door and knock. If anyone hears My voice and opens the door, I will come in to him and dine with him, and he with Me

NOTES

_____

_____

_____

_____

_____

_____

_____

_____

_____

_____

_____

_____

_____

_____

_____

_____

_____

_____

_____